SRa PHONICS 3

Alvin Granowsky, Ed.D.

CONTRIBUTING AUTHORS

Joy Ann Tweedt, classroom teacher
Norman Najimy, educational consultant

REVIEWERS

Dr. Helen Brown
Director of Elementary Programs, K-8
Metropolitan Public Schools
Nashville, Tennessee

Nora Forester
Associate Superintendent for Curriculum
Archdiocese of San Antonio and
Diocese of Victoria
San Antonio, Texas

Pamela K. Francis
Principal
Seltice Elementary School
Post Falls, Idaho

SRa

SRA/McGraw-Hill
Columbus, Ohio

Contents

ISBN 002-886011-2

12 13 14 15 DBH 06 05

CREDITS

Project Supervisor: Deborah Akers
Production Design and Development: PAT CUSICK and ASSOCIATES
Design Director: LESIAK/CRAMPTON DESIGN INC.

Beginning Consonants

1. 🗣 Say each picture name.
2. 👂 Listen to the first sound.
3. ✏️ Write the letter or letters that stand for the first sound.

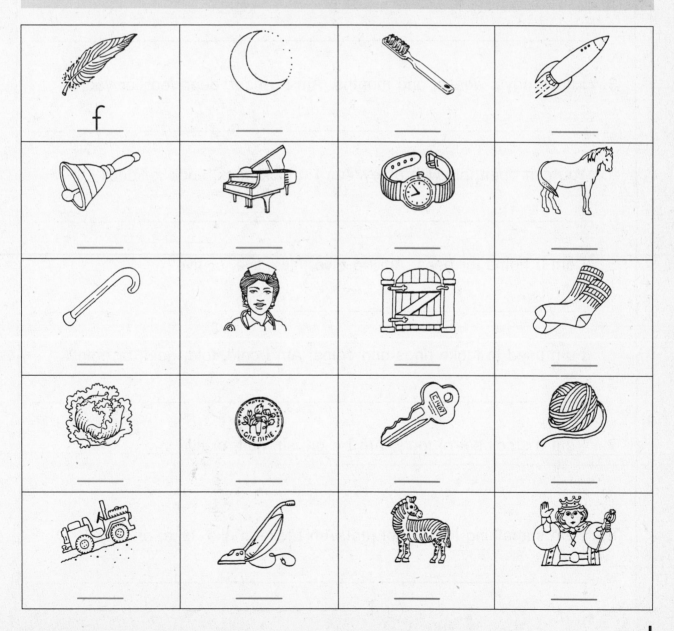

f

1 📖 Read each riddle.   2 ✏️ Circle the correct answer.
3 ✏️ Write the answer in a complete sentence.

1. I have a cover and pages. Am I a look, (book,) cook, or hook?

   A book has a cover and pages.

2. You can get this from the sun. Am I a van, pan, tan, or fan?

   _____

3. I have days, weeks, and months. Am I a near, dear, fear, or year?

   _____

4. You can open this with a key. Am I a lock, rock, sock, or dock?

   _____

5. I am a home for bees. Am I a dive, hive, live, or five?

   _____

6. I am used to make rings and coins. Am I cold, fold, gold, or hold?

   _____

7. I am a small set of tools. Am I a pit, sit, quit, or kit?

   _____

8. I am something that is not real. Am I fake, make, take, or bake?

   _____

Using language arts; writing sentences with words with consonant sounds in initial position

Ending Consonants

1. 🗣 Say each picture name.
2. 👂 Listen to the last sound.
3. ✏️ Write the letter that stands for the last sound.

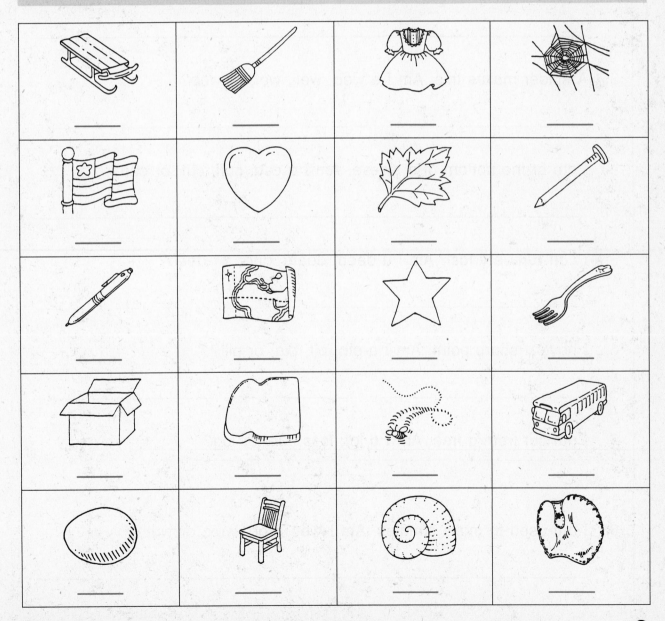

Introducing consonant sounds in final position

3

Ending Consonants

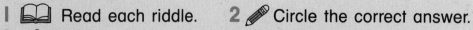

1 📖 Read each riddle.   2 ✏️ Circle the correct answer.
3 ✏️ Write the answer in a complete sentence.

1. I am a humming sound. Am I a bun, buzz, bud, or bug?

   _____

2. You can live in this. Am I a hut, hug, hum, or hub?

   _____

3. A spider makes this. Am I a wed, well, wet, or web?

   _____

4. I am at the bottom of a sleeve. Am I a cub, cuff, cut, or cud?

   _____

5. I can run very fast. Am I a deep, deem, deer, or deed?

   _____

6. I have a sharp point. Am I a pin, pit, pig, or pill?

   _____

7. I am cut from a tree. Am I a lot, loss, lob, or log?

   _____

8. I am used to make candles. Am I was, wag, wax, or wall?

   _____

Middle Consonants

1. 🗣 Say each picture name.
2. 👂 Listen to the middle sound.
3. ✏️ Write the letter that stands for the middle sound.

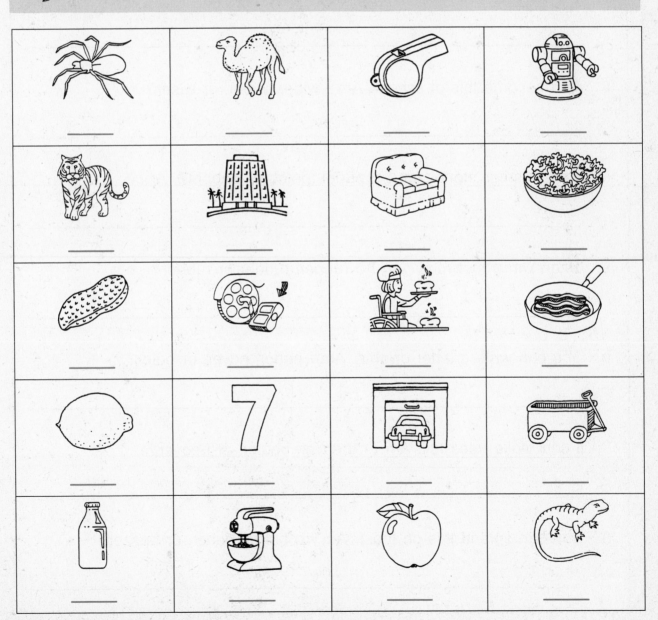

1 📖 Read each riddle.   **2** ✏️ Circle the correct answer.
3 ✏️ Write the answer in a complete sentence.

1. I have four wheels. Am I a woman, wagon, or waxen?

   _____

2. I am a beam of light. Am I a laser, later, or layer?

   _____

3. You become this at school. Am I wider, wiper, or wiser?

   _____

4. I am a small stone. Am I a pedal, petal, or pebble?

   _____

5. I can win a foot race. Am I a runner, rudder, or rubber?

   _____

6. You can write a letter on this. Am I paper, payer, or paler?

   _____

7. I can make trees fall. Am I a beaker, beater, or beaver?

   _____

8. You can spread this on toast. Am I a buffer, butter, or buzzer?

   _____

1 📖 Read each sentence and look at the picture.

2 ✏️ Write the letters that complete both words in the sentence.

1.  The artis **t** is painting a ___icture.

2.  The ra___io is playing a rock-and-roll ___ong.

3.  Mother is filling the tu___ with wa___er.

4.  The pa___ade passed by my ___ouse.

5. 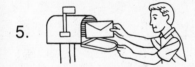 Todd put the car___ in the mailbo___.

6.  May I ___ickle you with a ___eather?

7.  ___ad put some mo___ey in the meter.

8.  Flowers and ___egetables grow in a ___arden.

9.  Linda got a pre___ent on her ___irthday.

10.  Ken has a boo___ about ___ets.

Consonants

Directions: Say each picture name.
Fill in the space next to the letter
that will complete the picture name.

Example

___uzzle

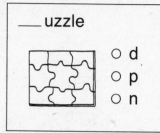

○ d
○ p
○ n

1. ___asket ○ m ○ b ○ v	2. wa___er ○ t ○ l ○ b	3. ho___ ○ b ○ p ○ c	4. ___esk ○ r ○ d ○ z
5. ba___ ○ g ○ v ○ d	6. ___et ○ d ○ p ○ j	7. bea___er ○ f ○ v ○ j	8. poo___ ○ l ○ s ○ m
9. shir___ ○ d ○ p ○ t	10. mu___ic ○ s ○ r ○ k	11. bar___ ○ g ○ n ○ m	12. fa___ily ○ r ○ s ○ m
13. ___adpole ○ t ○ m ○ b	14. wor___ ○ k ○ t ○ m	15. pa___er ○ j ○ p ○ w	16. ___ire ○ f ○ d ○ m
17. ___ar ○ c ○ h ○ f	18. ru___er ○ b ○ l ○ x	19. fu___ ○ h ○ r ○ t	20. ___andwich ○ j ○ z ○ s

8

Hard and Soft c

Why did the cat ask the waiter for a cheeseburger?

Because they were out of mice!

The letter **c** followed by **e**, **i**, or **y** usually stands for the soft sound of **c**.

mice

The letter **c** followed by any other letter usually stands for the hard sound of **c**.

cat

1 📖 Read each word.
2 👀 Look at the letter that comes after **c**. 3 ✌ Say the word.
4 ✏ Write the word under the sound of **c** you hear.

cub	rice	clam	lace	case	cute	cent	cane
city	crab	race	code	cider	ice	cave	cell

 Hard c

 Soft c

cub
_____   _____

_____   _____

_____   _____

_____   _____

_____   _____

Hard and Soft g

Name six animals.

Two goats and four giraffes!

The letter **g** followed by **e**, **i**, or **y** often stands for the soft sound of **g**.

giraffe

The letter **g** followed by any other letter usually stands for the hard sound of **g**.

goat

1 📖 Read each word.
2 👀 Look at the letter that comes after **g**. 3 🗣 Say the word.
4 ✏️ Write the word under the sound of **g** you hear.

| gate | gym | page | gold | gull | gem | stage | large |
| gave | cage | gone | huge | giant | goat | grade | flag |

Hard **g**   Soft **g**

_____   _____

_____   _____

_____   _____

_____   _____

_____   _____

_____   _____

_____   _____

10

Introducing the hard and soft sounds of **g**

1 📖 Read the story below.   2 🗣 Say each word.
3 👂 Listen for the hard and soft sounds of **c** and **g**.
4 ✏️ Circle the words that have the soft sound of **c** or **g**.
5 ✏️ Draw a line under the words that have the hard sound of **c** or **g**.
If a word has both a hard and soft **c** or **g**, circle it and underline it.

My uncle and I had a great time at the circus.

The clowns were funny. One raced around

a huge tiger in a cage. Then a girl rode

a bicycle and balanced a large cone on her nose.

A man and woman climbed up to a high wire.

The man held a giant pole as he

carefully walked across. The woman sat

in the center. The crowd screamed and clapped

like crazy. It was certainly fun!

1 📖 Read each question about the story.
2 ✏️ Fill in the space by the correct answer.

1. Where did this story happen?
   ● at the circus
   ○ at a dance
   ○ at a bicycle race

2. Who raced around a tiger?
   ○ a girl
   ○ an uncle
   ○ a clown

3. Where did the man walk?
   ○ around a cage
   ○ across a high wire
   ○ on a giant pole

4. Which is the best title for this story?
   ○ "The Funny Clown"
   ○ "Fun at the Circus"
   ○ "My Uncle"

1 📖 Read each sentence.

2 ✏️ Circle the sound of **c** or **g** that you hear in the underlined word.

		Hard **c** (**c**=**k**)	Soft **c** (**c**=**s**)
1.	Please cut me a <u>slice</u> of bread.	k	ⓢ
2.	The rabbit ate the <u>carrot</u>.	k	s
3.	The prize cost ten <u>cents</u>.	k	s
4.	It is <u>cold</u> in winter.	k	s
5.	We can put a <u>cap</u> on the bottle.	k	s
6.	The team is in last <u>place</u>.	k	s

		Hard **g** (**g**=**g**)	Soft **g** (**g**=**j**)
1.	I cannot find the <u>page</u> number.	g	j
2.	The frog ate a <u>huge</u> bug.	g	j
3.	Gordon fixed the <u>game</u> with tape.	g	j
4.	The <u>giant</u> was very large.	g	j
5.	She <u>began</u> five years ago.	g	j
6.	My <u>dog</u> can do tricks.	g	j

Hard and Soft **c** and **g**

Directions: Read each word. Fill in the space next to the letter that stands for the sound of **c** or **g**.

Example

cut   ○ k
     ○ s

1. city ○ k ○ s	2. game ○ g ○ j	3. giant ○ g ○ j	4. ice ○ k ○ s
5. large ○ g ○ j	6. second ○ k ○ s	7. ago ○ g ○ j	8. orange ○ g ○ j
9. center ○ k ○ s	10. gym ○ g ○ j	11. camp ○ k ○ s	12. gold ○ g ○ j
13. color ○ k ○ s	14. began ○ g ○ j	15. village ○ g ○ j	16. face ○ k ○ s
17. cold ○ k ○ s	18. nice ○ k ○ s	19. gate ○ g ○ j	20. carrot ○ k ○ s

Testing the hard and soft sounds of **c** and **g**; using an adapted standardized test format

Short Vowels: **a**

Act 1: Sam in "Animals and Ants"

1 Say each picture name.   2 Listen for the short sound of **a**.
3 Circle the word for the picture name.

nap (pan) pat mat	and ask tan ant	bat bad tab fat	fan nap fat can
lap lad cap cab	tag rag nag sag	can sat van ran	ant sad pad add

1 Say each picture name.   2 Listen for the short sound of **a**.
3 Find the word in the box and write it on the line.

ham   hat   ram   tag   gas   map   wag   man

map	_____	_____	_____
_____	_____	_____	_____

14

1 📖 Read each sentence, saying the picture names.
2 ✏️ Write the sentence, changing the pictures to words.

1. Dan left the 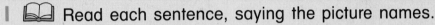 in the  .

   Dan left the map in the van.

2. The took a nap on my .

   _____

3. Pam to the .

   _____

4. Dad put the 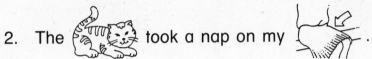 in the  .

   _____

5. Jan sat on a  next to a .

   _____

6. Sam tied a on the .

   _____

7. The  blew air on the .

   _____

Short Vowels: i

Fish Pig Tick Iguana Chick

1 🗣 Say each picture name. 2 👂 Listen for the short sound of **i**.
3 ✏️ Circle the word for the picture name.

big pin pig gap	rid rib cab bib	fan fit bin fin	lip lap lit sip
lad lid did lip	hat him hit sit	bit mitt mat quit	hill pill fill hall

1 🗣 Say each picture name. 2 👂 Listen for the short sound of **i**.
3 ✏️ Find the word in the box and write it on the line.

kit   pit   win   wig   tip   bib   rip   dig

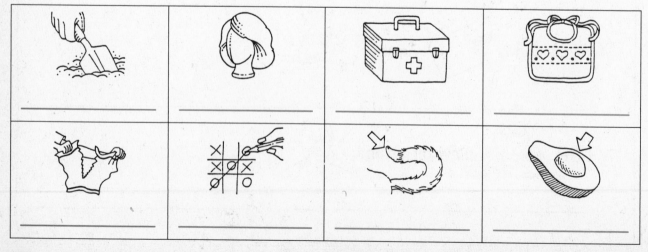

Introducing the short sound of **i**

> 1 📖 Read each sentence, saying the picture names.
> 2 ✏️ Write the sentence, changing the pictures to words.

1. Kim fixed the 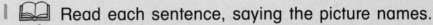 with a  .

_____

2. The 🐷 liked to 🖐️ in the mud.

_____

3. A 🐟 has a 🦈 to swim.

_____

4. The 🧰 did not fit on the 🪟 .

_____

5. Jim ⚾ the ball with the 🪶 of the bat.

_____

6. The 🍲 is too big for the 🍽️ .

_____

7. I saw 6 sails on the ⛵ .

_____

1 📖 Read the words in the box.   2 ✌ Say each word.
3 👂 Listen for the short sound of **a** or **i**.
4 ✏ Write each word under the correct heading and
next to its vowel sound.

lip	mat	crib	hand	ask	sit	sad	fan	back	hip
nap	fix	glass	rib	mad	dish	bad	ill	dig	glad

Things You Can Do

1. (**a**) _____ask_____

2. (**i**) _____

3. (**a**) _____

4. (**i**) _____

5. (**i**) _____

Things Inside a House

1. (**a**) _____

2. (**i**) _____

3. (**a**) _____

4. (**a**) _____

5. (**i**) _____

Ways You Can Feel

1. (**a**) _____

2. (**a**) _____

3. (**a**) _____

4. (**i**) _____

5. (**a**) _____

Parts of Your Body

1. (**i**) _____

2. (**a**) _____

3. (**a**) _____

4. (**i**) _____

5. (**i**) _____

18

Short Vowels: o

Sam Mops the Prop Shop

1 🗣 Say each picture name.   2 👂 Listen for the short sound of **o**.
3 ✏️ Circle the word for the picture name.

hop map pop mop	pot tip top tap	cot hot cat cod	fix fox box fog
pat pit pot top	log lot hog lit	pad nod pod pop	dig dog jog dot

1 🗣 Say each picture name.   2 👂 Listen for the short sound of **o**.
3 ✏️ Find the word in the box and write it on the line.

dot   box   fog   cob   nod   rod   hop   jog

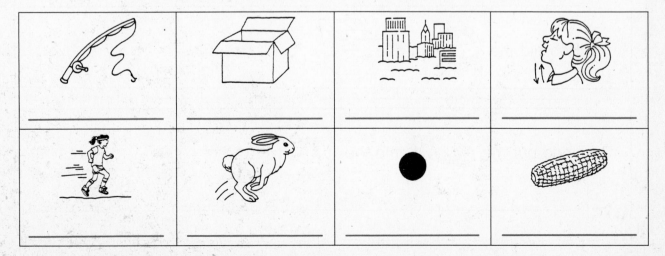

Introducing the short sound of **o**

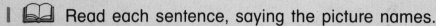 Read each sentence, saying the picture names.

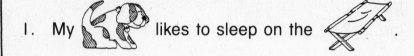 Write the sentence, changing the pictures to words.

1. My ![dog] likes to sleep on the ![cot] .

_____

2. Don cleaned the ![spot] with a ![mop] .

_____

3. The ![frog] got ![hot] in the sun.

_____

4. Mom likes to ![jog] in the ![city] .

_____

5. The ![ox] did not stop at the ![log] .

_____

6. Bob hid the ![top] in a ![box] .

_____

7. Todd put the ![corn] into the ![pot] .

_____

1 Say each picture name.   **2** Listen for the short sound of **e**.
3 Circle the word for the picture name.

jot jet jam get	leg log beg let	red bad bed bit	ball bill tell bell
web wed wet fed	pit pet pot met	not nap net set	pin pan den pen

1 Say each picture name.   **2** Listen for the short sound of **e**.
3 Find the word in the box and write it on the line.

egg   hen   fell   ten   men   beg   vet   wet

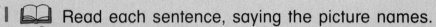 Read each sentence, saying the picture names.

Write the sentence, changing the pictures to words.

1. The two  met on a .

_____

2. The  sat on an in the nest.

_____

3. Did your _____ get _____ in the rain?

_____

4. The _____ tried to _____ the pup.

_____

5. Fred put a _____ on his _____ .

_____

6. Beth saw a _____ under the _____ .

_____

7. There were fish in the .

_____

Using language arts; writing sentences with words with the short sound of **e**

Short Vowels: reviewing a, e, i, o

1 📖 Read the words in the box. 2 🗣 Say each word.
3 👂 Listen for the short sound of **a**, **e**, **i**, or **o**.
4 ✏️ Write each word under the correct heading and
next to its vowel sound.

| web | hop | pal | bib | skip | log | hat | dress | Mom | ran |
| kid | nest | jog | wig | Dad | swim | cap | men | twig | grass |

Ways People Move

1. (**o**) _____

2. (**i**) _____

3. (**a**) _____

4. (**o**) _____

5. (**i**) _____

Things You Can Wear

1. (**i**) _____

2. (**a**) _____

3. (**e**) _____

4. (**i**) _____

5. (**a**) _____

Names for People

1. (**a**) _____

2. (**o**) _____

3. (**i**) _____

4. (**a**) _____

5. (**e**) _____

Things in the Woods

1. (**e**) _____

2. (**o**) _____

3. (**e**) _____

4. (**i**) _____

5. (**a**) _____

Short Vowels: **u**

UGH!! Hundreds of bugs! RUN!

1 🔊 Say each picture name. **2** 👂 Listen for the short sound of **u**.
3 ✏️ Circle the word for the picture name.

but hum tab tub	bus bug sub bud	jog jug dug jet	cap cub cut cup
bun fun ban bin	net not nut hut	rag rug rub hug	rut rot sun run

1 🔊 Say each picture name. **2** 👂 Listen for the short sound of **u**.
3 ✏️ Find the word in the box and write it on the line.

mug   hut   mud   pup   tug   bug   sub   bud

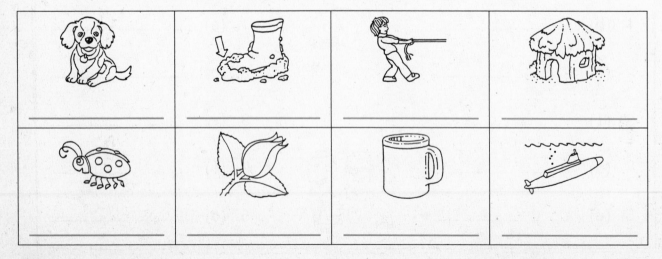

24

> 1 📖 Read each sentence, saying the picture names.
> 2 ✏️ Write the sentence, changing the pictures to words.

1. Jill had to to get on the .

_____

2. Dad got a new for the .

_____

3. The took a nap in the .

_____

4. We washed the off the  .

_____

5. Len had a  of milk and a  .

_____

6. Gus played the 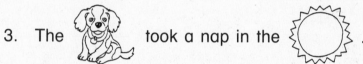 in the  .

_____

7. There was a on the  .

_____

1 📖 Read the words in the box.   2 🗣 Say each word.
3 👂 Listen for the short vowel sound.
4 ✏️ Write each word under the correct heading and
next to its vowel sound.

| cab | hill | egg | fox | cat | chop | van | club | fig | sub |
| hen | nut | hut | bus | ham | pig | | den | jet | ox | camp |

Things You Can Eat

1. (e) _____

2. (o) _____

3. (i) _____

4. (u) _____

5. (a) _____

Things You Can Ride In

1. (a) _____

2. (a) _____

3. (u) _____

4. (u) _____

5. (e) _____

Kinds of Animals

1. (o) _____

2. (a) _____

3. (e) _____

4. (i) _____

5. (o) _____

Places You Can Go

1. (i) _____

2. (u) _____

3. (u) _____

4. (e) _____

5. (a) _____

26

Unit review: writing words with short vowel sounds; categorizing

1 📖 Read each riddle.

2 ✏️ Choose the answer from the box and write it on the line.

sun	job	well	quit	map
red	fun	sad	mop	hill

1. I am not happy. _____sad_____

2. I am used for cleaning the floor. _____

3. I am something that shines. _____

4. I gave up and stopped trying. _____

5. I show roads and cities. _____

6. I am a beautiful color. _____

7. I am a hole made to get water or oil. _____

8. I am work that has to be done. _____

9. I am not as high as a mountain. _____

10. I am a good time. _____

Short Vowels

Directions: Say each picture name.
Listen to the vowel sound. Fill in the space
next to the word for the picture name.

Example

○ big
○ bag
○ bug

1. ○ pin ○ pan ○ pen	**2.** ○ rug ○ rig ○ rag	**3.** ○ cab ○ cob ○ cub	**4.** ○ pop ○ pep ○ pup
5. ○ dig ○ dog ○ dug	**6.** ○ bed ○ bud ○ bad	**7.** ○ him ○ hum ○ ham	**8.** ○ ten ○ tin ○ ton
9. ○ hut ○ hit ○ hot	**10.** ○ fin ○ fun ○ fan	**11.** ○ rid ○ rod ○ red	**12.** ○ rib ○ rob ○ rub
13. ○ pot ○ pit ○ pat	**14.** ○ mud ○ mad ○ mid	**15.** ○ nut ○ not ○ net	**16.** ○ cot ○ cut ○ cat
17. ○ log ○ leg ○ lag	**18.** ○ lad ○ lid ○ led	**19.** ○ bun ○ bin ○ ban	**20.** ○ bit ○ but ○ bat

Testing short vowel sounds; using an adapted standardized test format

Long Vowels: ā

When a word has two vowels, and one is final **e**, the first vowel is long and the **e** is silent.

plān¢

When two vowels are together, the first vowel is usually long and the second is silent.

rāi̸n

When **y** follows the vowel **a**, the **y** is silent and the **a** is long.

dāy̸

1 📖 Read the words in the box. 2 ✏️ Write each word under its spelling pattern. 3 ✏️ Mark the letters as shown.

| way | nail | race | say | wait | made | pay | bake | tail |
| name | mail | ray | bait | cave | may | main | late | bay |

 _ ā _ ¢ = ā

 ā i̸ = ā

 ā y̸ = ā

rāc¢

Introducing the long sound of **a**

29

1 📖 Read each sentence.
2 ✏️ Circle the words that make sense in the sentence.

1. Dad put white (paint) on the front ~~gain~~
   ~~pane~~ (gate) .

2. The sky is grain when it rails
   gray   rains .

3. We walked down a trail to the lay
   trace   lake .

4. Kay main a plate out of clay
   made   claim .

5. Jake wants to play a gave of chess.
   place   game

6. Dave pave three dollars for the tape
   paid   tame .

7. Jane saw her name on a letter in the mail
   nail   maid .

8. My friend will not way if I am lane
   wait   late .

9. The faces of the twins looked the same
   fails   sail .

10. The picture of the cave is on pail five.
    came   page

Using language arts; using sentence context to select words with the long sound of **a**

Long Vowels: ī

HIDE! Lie down in the vines!

When a word has two vowels, and one is final **e**, the first vowel is long and the **e** is silent.

hīd¢

When two vowels are together, the first vowel is usually long and the second is silent.

lī¢

| 📖 Read the words in the box.　2 ✏️ Write each word under its spelling pattern.　3 ✏️ Mark the letters as shown.

nice	die	side	pie	wife	like
tie	line	pipe	lie	mile	nine

_ ī _ ¢ = ī   _ ī¢ = ī

1 📖 Read each sentence.

2 ✏️ Circle the words that make sense in the sentence.

1. Mike rode one mile / mice on his bite / bike .

2. The hide / hike will begin at nice / nine o'clock.

3. Can you tie / tile the fishing like / line in a knot?

4. Please hike / hide the present behind the pile / pike .

5. Mother drives / dimes on the right side / slice of the road.

6. Jill took a bike / bite of the slice of pine / pie .

7. The red kite / lie with the long tail is mile / mine .

8. I paid the file / fine with my last two dies / dimes .

9. The grapes on the vine / vice are very rice / ripe .

10. The nice / nine lady always slides / smiles at me.

Using language arts; using sentence context to select words with the long sound of **i**

1 📖 Read the words in the box. 2 🗣 Say each word.
3 👂 Listen for the long sound of **a** or **i**.
4 ✏️ Write each word under the correct heading and
next to its vowel sound.

fine	play	dates	nice	pipe	dive	grapes
vain	hike	pie	wise	race	lime	brave
tray	skate	vase	rice	plate	knife	

Things You Can Eat

1. (ā) _dates_

2. (ā) _____

3. (ī) _____

4. (ī) _____

5. (ī) _____

Things You Can Do

1. (ā) _____

2. (ī) _____

3. (ī) _____

4. (ā) _____

5. (ā) _____

Things Inside a House

1. (ī) _____

2. (ā) _____

3. (ā) _____

4. (ā) _____

5. (ī) _____

Ways You Can Act

1. (ī) _____

2. (ī) _____

3. (ā) _____

4. (ī) _____

5. (ā) _____

Reviewing the long sounds of **a** and **i**; categorizing

Long Vowels: ō

OH NO! The hoe made a hole in the boat!

When a word has two vowels, and one is final **e**, the first vowel is long and the **e** is silent.

hōl¢

When two vowels are together, the first vowel is usually long and the second is silent.

bō¢t   hō¢

I 📖 Read the words in the box.   2 ✏️ Write each word under its spelling pattern.   3 ✏️ Mark the letters as shown.

toe	road	robe	hoe	joke	toad	rose	coat	woke
bone	doe	note	moan	foe	goat	home	soap	nose

 _ ō _ ¢ = ō

 ō¢ = ō

 ō¢ = ō

Introducing the long sound of **o**

1 📖 Read each sentence.

2 ✏️ Circle the words that make sense in the sentence.

1. Joan tied the   rope   to the   poke   .
                    rode   pole

2. Our dog dug a   hoe   for its   boat   .
                 hole   bone

3. Joe   broke   his   tone   when he fell.
        boat   toe

4. Kim smelled the red   rode   with her   nose   .
                     rose   note

5. Moe took a   boat   to his   home   on the lake.
            broke   hole

6. We saw a small   toast   hopping down the   road   .
              toad   role

7. The heavy   stone   did not   foe   in the water.
           slope   float

8. Lisa left the   nope   in the pocket of her   coat   .
            note   coal

9. Bob   woke   up and put on his new   rode   .
        wove   robe

10. Dad used a   home   and some   sole   to wash the car.
             hose   soap

Long Vowels: ē

When two vowels are together, the first vowel is usually long and the second is silent.

strē¢t   bē∅n

1 📖 Read the words in the box.   2 ✏️ Write each word under its spelling pattern.   3 ✏️ Mark the letters as shown.

feel	read	week	bee	team	need	mean	seal	deep	meet
leap	heel	tea	seem	keep	seat	seed	meal	real	each

ē¢ = ē

ē∅ = ē

Long Vowels: ē

1 📖 Read each sentence.

2 ✏️ Circle the words that make sense in the sentence.

1. Have you seen / seam that green lead / leaf on the tree?

2. Jean likes to each / eat meat and beaks / beans .

3. The heap / heat of the sun made me feel / feed weak.

4. The team / tea had four games this week / weed .

5. Each / Eat year Dean plants seats / seeds in the garden.

6. Some beets / bees have a hive in that peel / tree .

7. Many fish live down deep / deal in the seam / sea .

8. The queen drank some teen / tea after her mean / meal .

9. Mom's feet / feel hurt when she wears high heats / heels .

10. Have you seem / seen the baby seats / seals ?

Long Vowels: reviewing
ā, ē, ī, ō

1 📖 Read the words in the box. 2 🗣 Say each word.
3 👂 Listen for the long sound of **a**, **e**, **i**, or **o**.
4 ✏️ Write each word under the correct heading and
next to its vowel sound.

queen	face	hoe	lake	vine	feet	bride
bay	weed	street	hose	toe	road	coach
rake	heel	maid	drive	wife	nose	

Things in a Garden

1. (ō) _____

2. (ī) _____

3. (ē) _____

4. (ō) _____

5. (ā) _____

Parts of Your Body

1. (ā) _____

2. (ē) _____

3. (ō) _____

4. (ē) _____

5. (ō) _____

Names for People

1. (ē) _____

2. (ī) _____

3. (ō) _____

4. (ā) _____

5. (ī) _____

Places on a Map

1. (ā) _____

2. (ā) _____

3. (ē) _____

4. (ō) _____

5. (ī) _____

38

Long Vowels: ū

When a word has two vowels, and one is final **e**, the first vowel is long and the **e** is silent.

hūg¢

When two vowels are together, the first vowel is usually long and the second is silent.

frū/t   clū¢

That huge flute is a clue...

I 📖 Read the words in the box.   2 ✏️ Write each word under its spelling pattern.   3 ✏️ Mark the letters as shown.

flute	blue	cue	tune	suit	true	mule	due
fruit	glue	prune	cruise	cube	juice	tube	bruise

 _ ū _ ¢ = ū    _ ū/ _ = ū    _ ū¢ = ū

_____   _____   _____

_____   _____   _____

_____   _____   _____

_____   _____   _____

_____   _____   _____

_____

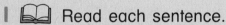

1 📖 Read each sentence.
2 ✏️ Circle the word that makes sense in the sentence.

1. Please put the ice   cube / cute   in my glass.

2. We sang that   tube / tune   in music class.

3. There is some ripe   fruit / fuse   on the table.

4. The library book is   due / dune   on Monday.

5. Dave wears a   sue / suit   and tie to work.

6. There is a very   huge / dude   lion in the zoo.

7. The can of sticky   true / glue   spilled on the rug.

8. The   cube / cute   little kitten played with the string.

9. June sat on the sand   dune / duke   at the beach.

10. A pipe and a   tune / tube   can look alike.

40

1 📖 Read the words in the box. 2 🗣 Say each word.
3 👂 Listen for the long vowel sound.
4 ✏️ Write each word under the correct heading and
next to its vowel sound.

cape	fruit	toad	jeep	beads	mule	train
toast	plane	mice	tie	rice	bike	suit
seal	meat	boat	robe	snake	grape	

Things You Can Wear

1. ($\bar{a}$) _____

2. ($\bar{e}$) _____

3. ($\bar{i}$) _____

4. ($\bar{u}$) _____

5. ($\bar{o}$) _____

Kinds of Animals

1. ($\bar{o}$) _____

2. ($\bar{u}$) _____

3. ($\bar{i}$) _____

4. ($\bar{e}$) _____

5. ($\bar{a}$) _____

Ways to Travel

1. ($\bar{e}$) _____

2. ($\bar{a}$) _____

3. ($\bar{a}$) _____

4. ($\bar{i}$) _____

5. ($\bar{o}$) _____

Things You Can Eat

1. ($\bar{u}$) _____

2. ($\bar{o}$) _____

3. ($\bar{i}$) _____

4. ($\bar{e}$) _____

5. ($\bar{a}$) _____

Unit review: writing words with long vowel sounds; categorizing

41

1 📖 Read each riddle.
2 ✏️ Choose the answer from the box and write it on the line.

joke	lie	hay	rain	toe	seal
time	week	vane	juice	flute	soap

1. You can play a tune on this. _____ flute _____

2. I tell which way the wind is blowing. _____

3. I am measured by a clock. _____

4. I am a part of the foot. _____

5. I have seven days. _____

6. Cows and horses like to eat this. _____

7. I am very good to drink. _____

8. I am a short, funny story. _____

9. I help make the flowers grow. _____

10. I make bubbles when mixed with water. _____

11. I am an animal that lives in the sea. _____

12. I am not the truth. _____

42

Long Vowels

Directions: Say each picture name.
Listen to the vowel sound. Fill in the space
next to the word for the picture name.

Example

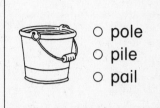

○ pole
○ pile
○ pail

1. ○ cave ○ cone ○ coat	2. ○ toe ○ tie ○ tile	3. ○ rail ○ race ○ ray	4. ○ gleam ○ glue ○ green
5. ○ goat ○ gate ○ game	6. ○ bake ○ beak ○ bike	7. ○ real ○ rain ○ rule	8. ○ rose ○ road ○ rice
9. ○ tea ○ toe ○ tube	10. ○ bee ○ base ○ boat	11. ○ loaf ○ leaf ○ life	12. ○ seed ○ seat ○ suit
13. ○ flute ○ float ○ fruit	14. ○ nine ○ nose ○ need	15. ○ cane ○ cage ○ cute	16. ○ deep ○ dive ○ dime
17. ○ toad ○ tail ○ time	18. ○ soap ○ sail ○ save	19. ○ huge ○ hive ○ hose	20. ○ bean ○ bone ○ bite

Testing long vowel sounds; using an adapted standardized test format

Reviewing Long and Short Vowels

ACT FIVE: "Agents Jake and Kay Save the Day"

Help me, PLEASE!

DANGER QUICKSAND

1 📖 Read the words in the box.   2 🗣 Say each word.
3 👂 Listen to the vowel sound.
4 ✏️ Write the word under the vowel sound you hear.

red	cab	bean	if	rub	same	box	fin	log	lay
jet	bone	tie	life	cube	gave	feel	job	us	had
see	mile	rain	road	huge	fan	week	cuff	lid	tell
ice	joke	tug	mule	yet	will	glue	toe	heat	soap
pig	nut	wait	map	less	kite	due	top	bat	hot

a   **e**   **i**   **o**   **u**

cab

ā   **ē**   **ī**   **ō**   **ū**

Reviewing long and short vowel sounds

1 📖 Read each sentence.
2 ✏️ Change the vowel sound in the underlined word to make a word that will complete the sentence.
3 ✏️ Write the new word on the line.

1. Ron <u>will</u> get some water from the ___well___ .

2. Tie a <u>rope</u> around this case of _____ apples.

3. Can you <u>read</u> the _____ sign from here?

4. Jill wore a wide <u>hat</u> in the _____ sun.

5. The huge ball was too <u>big</u> to fit into the _____ .

6. Tim rode one <u>mile</u> on his pet _____ .

7. After the <u>race</u> Mimi ate a hot bowl of _____ .

8. How much did you <u>pay</u> for that slice of _____ ?

9. Gail used the <u>tip</u> of her pencil to _____ the beat.

10. After school we like to play <u>tug</u> of war and _____ .

11. Pam went for a <u>sail</u> and saw a _____ swim by.

12. Ben hurt his <u>leg</u> when he fell over the _____ .

1 📖 Read the story below.   2 🗣 Say each word.
3 👂 Listen carefully to the vowel sounds.
4 ✏️ Draw a line under each word with a long vowel sound.

Did you ever spend a <u>day</u> at the lake?
There are many ways to have fun.

It is fun to dive into the water and take a swim.
You can float on your back and look at the clouds.
Then you can play in the sand on the beach.

You can sail in a boat on the lake.
The wind will push the sails and take you for a ride.
Bring a fishing rod and some bait if you like to fish.
Fish are good to eat and make a fine meal.

You can hike around the lake. On the trail you may see pine cones,
spider webs, huge trees with green leaves, butterflies, and bees.

A day at the lake can be lots of fun!

1 📖 Read each question about the story.
2 ✏️ Fill in the space by the correct answer.

1. Where can you dive and float?
   ○ on a trail
   ● in the lake
   ○ on the beach
   ○ in the sky

2. Why would you need
   a rod and bait?
   ○ to hike
   ○ to swim
   ○ to fish
   ○ to sail

3. What won't you see on the trail?
   ○ bees
   ○ pine cones
   ○ huge trees
   ○ fish

4. Which is the best title for
   this story?
   ○ "Eating Fish"
   ○ "A Rainy Day"
   ○ "Fun at the Lake"
   ○ "The Long Hike"

Unit review: reading a story with words with long and short vowel sounds; story comprehension

Long and Short Vowels

Directions: Read the word in the box. Listen to the vowel sound. Fill in the space below the word with the same vowel sound as the word in the box.

Example

ham	hail ○	man ○	hay ○

1. rain	ran ○	rag ○	pail ○		12. hoe	hop ○	pot ○	home ○
2. hid	hide ○	hike ○	did ○		13. due	dune ○	rub ○	dug ○
3. joke	job ○	toe ○	jog ○		14. sad	sale ○	ham ○	say ○
4. feet	feel ○	fell ○	ten ○		15. like	lie ○	lip ○	kit ○
5. tub	tune ○	tube ○	nut ○		16. bet	team ○	beat ○	beg ○
6. lot	loan ○	log ○	tone ○		17. tube	tug ○	tune ○	but ○
7. day	date ○	had ○	hat ○		18. peak	keep ○	pet ○	pep ○
8. rose	rob ○	soap ○	rot ○		19. lie	lit ○	lime ○	pin ○
9. tell	tea ○	leap ○	ten ○		20. make	mail ○	mad ○	can ○
10. nail	name ○	nap ○	lap ○		21. dime	did ○	mill ○	die ○
11. got	goal ○	hog ○	hole ○		22. weed	wed ○	seat ○	set ○

Testing long and short vowel sounds; using an adapted standardized test format

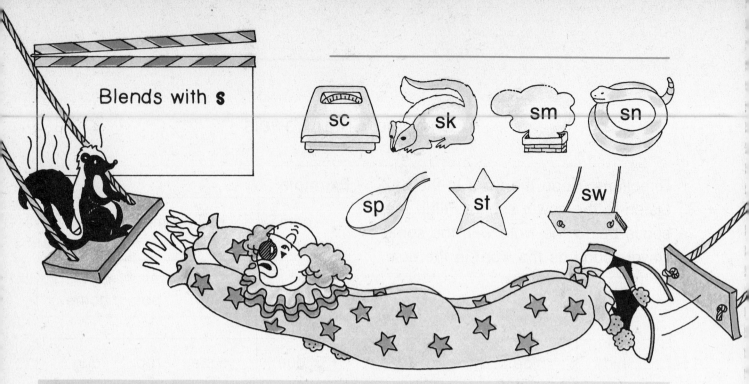

Blends with s

sc   sk   sm   sn   sp   st   sw

1   Say each picture name.
2   Listen to the blend at the beginning.
3   Find the word in the box and write it on the line.
4   Circle the letters for the blend.

spin	stage	swim	spider	skip	smile
scoop	snow	stove	skate	sweep	snail

Blends with l

| bl | cl | fl |
| gl | pl | sl |

1 👁 Say each picture name.
2 👂 Listen to the blend at the beginning.
3 ✏ Find the word in the box and write it on the line.
4 ✏ Circle the letters for the blend.

| globe | sled | plug | float | glass | blanket |
| clip | sleeve | cloud | blouse | flute | plane |

Blends with r

1. 🗣 Say each picture name.
2. 👂 Listen to the blend at the beginning.
3. ✏️ Find the word in the box and write it on the line.
4. ✏️ Circle the letters for the blend.

grill	fruit	broom	frame	drum	crab
bread	drill	truck	grass	prince	tree

1	📖 Read each sentence.
2	✏️ Circle the word that makes sense in the sentence.
3	✏️ Write it on the line.

1. The pretty flowers _____smell_____ so sweet.
   swell   spell   (smell)

2. Fran knows how to _____ the flute.
   play   clay   gray

3. It is easy to _____ eggs in butter.
   cry   fry   spy

4. Do you know the _____ of the game?
   store   score   snore

5. We went on a _____ on the train.
   trip   flip   drip

6. Meg took her _____ to the ice rink.
   states   slates   skates

7. The _____ will fix the broken cup.
   clue   glue   blue

8. Your _____ is used for thinking.
   brain   grain   stain

9. There is only a _____ of milk in the glass.
   prop   crop   drop

1 📖 Read each underlined word and change the blend to make the word that names the picture.

2 ✏️ Write the new word on the line.

sc	sk	sn	sm		bl	cl	fl		br	cr	dr	fr
sp	st	sw			gl	pl	sl		gr	pr	tr	

1. Change **tr**ail to

   snail

2. Change **pl**ate to

   _____

3. Change **pr**ess to

   _____

4. Change **sm**og to

   _____

5. Change **sp**ill to

   _____

6. Change **cl**ove to

   _____

7. Change **cr**y to

   _____

8. Change **sl**ip to

   _____

9. Change **br**ing to

   _____

10. Change **br**ain to

    _____

11. Change **bl**ue to

    _____

12. Change **sn**ag to

    _____

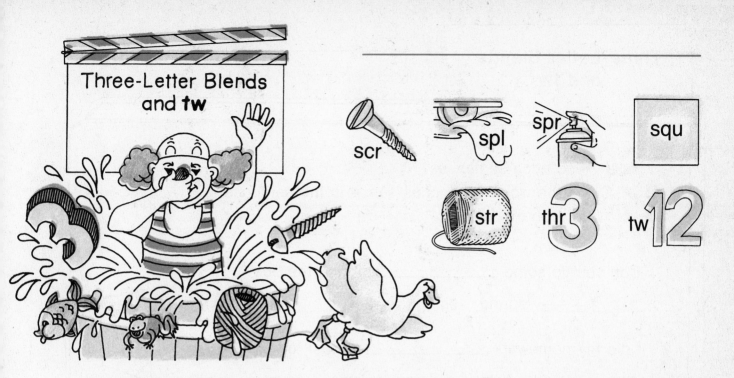

Three-Letter Blends and **tw**

scr spl spr squ

str thr 3 tw 12

1. 🗣 Say each picture name.
2. 👂 Listen to the blend at the beginning.
3. ✏️ Find the word in the box and write it on the line.
4. ✏️ Circle the letters for the blend.

thread	twins	squeeze	throw	screen	street
split	spread	splinter	squirrel	twig	scream

1 📖 Read each sentence.
2 ✏️ Circle the word that makes sense in the sentence.
3 ✏️ Write it on the line.

1. Can you tie some _____ around the box?

spring   string   swing

2. I did my homework _____ as fast today.

twice   splice   spice

3. If you are in trouble, _____ for help.

cream   stream   scream

4. Mindy broke the _____ on her bag.

trap   strap   scrap

5. We heard the _____ of the rusty door hinge.

speak   streak   squeak

6. The _____ wear the same clothes.

twins   spins   grins

7. Pam fixed the rip with a needle and _____ .

spread   thread   bread

8. Dad has to _____ the paint on the wall.

spray   stray   tray

9. The rock hit the water with a big _____ .

trash   thrash   splash

Using language arts; using sentence context to select words with three-letter blends or **tw**

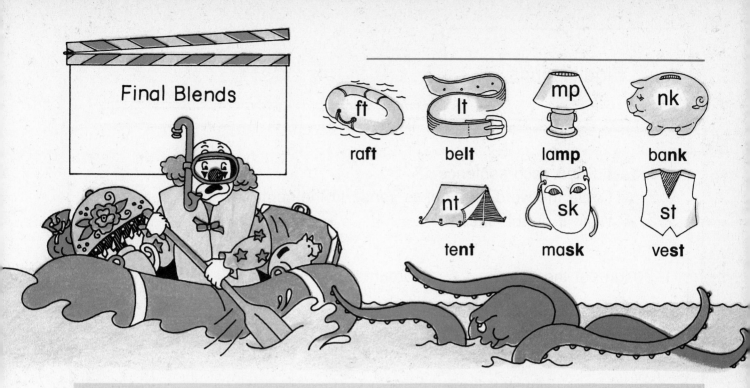

Final Blends

ra**ft**

be**lt**

la**mp**

ba**nk**

te**nt**

ma**sk**

ve**st**

1. 🗣 Say each picture name.
2. 👂 Listen to the blend at the end.
3. ✏️ Find the word in the box and write it on the line.
4. ✏️ Circle the letters for the blend.

| wink | ramp | salt | quilt | desk | gift |
| tusk | cent | sink | toast | dump | paint |

Introducing consonant blends in final position: **ft**, **lt**, **mp**, **nk**, **nt**, **sk**, **st**

Final Blends

1 📖 Read each sentence.
2 ✏️ Circle the word that makes sense in the sentence.
3 ✏️ Write it on the line.

1. Jean put the _____ around her waist.

   best   belt   bent

2. Eric pulled the _____ off each ear of corn.

   husk   hunt   hunk

3. Liz floated down the river on her _____ .

   rank   ramp   raft

4. At camp I sleep in the top _____ .

   bump   bunk   bust

5. Mom threw away the old _____ .

   junk   jump   just

6. We must sweep the _____ off the floor.

   dunk   dusk   dust

7. Did you make a _____ of what you want?

   lift   list   link

8. Rosa had to _____ for her lost shoe.

   hunt   hunk   husk

9. Tim wore a funny _____ to the party.

   malt   mast   mask

Using language arts; using sentence context to select words with blends in final position

1 📖 Read each underlined word and change the blend to make the word that names the picture.

2 ✏️ Write the new word on the line.

scr	spl	ft	mp	str	nt	tw
spr	squ	lt	nk	thr	st	sk

1. Change de**nt** to

_____

2. Change **squ**aw to

_____

3. Change la**st** to

_____

4. Change **spr**ig to

_____

5. Change **thr**ash to

_____

6. Change **squ**irt to

_____

7. Change sa**nk** to

_____

8. Change **str**eam to

_____

9. Change si**ft** to

_____

10. Change **spr**ead to

_____

11. Change **str**ing to

_____

12. Change ra**mp** to

_____

1 📖 Read the words in the box. 2 📖 Read each clue.

3 ✏️ Write the correct word in the puzzle.

front	print
mask	twist
stripes	square
closed	spilt
slant	blink
plant	three
drift	stamp
skunk	

ACROSS

2. This is not the back.
5. This can make a strong smell.
6. This means to wind around.
9. This shape has four sides.
10. This can be a flower or tree.
11. This means to flash on and off.
12. The milk was ___ on the floor.

DOWN

1. This is a way to make letters.
3. This can be a big pile of snow.
4. This is not open.
5. You buy this at the post office.
6. This is one more than two.
7. A ramp is sloped like this.
8. This covers your face.
9. Zebras have these.

Unit review: using words with consonant blends to complete a crossword puzzle

Consonant Blends

Directions: Fill in the space next to the blend that will complete the word.

Example

___ider
- ○ sp
- ○ st
- ○ sk

1. ___ale ○ sl ○ sm ○ sc	2. ___ush ○ br ○ pr ○ fr	3. dri___ ○ st ○ ft ○ lt	4. ___oat ○ scr ○ thr ○ str
5. ___ad ○ bl ○ fl ○ gl	6. la___ ○ sk ○ mp ○ nt	7. ___ing ○ spr ○ thr ○ scr	8. ___all ○ sk ○ sm ○ sn
9. ___ong ○ spr ○ str ○ scr	10. a___ ○ st ○ sk ○ lt	11. ___it ○ spl ○ spr ○ scr	12. ___eak ○ scr ○ spr ○ squ
13. a___ ○ lt ○ nt ○ mp	14. ___ice ○ fr ○ tw ○ sw	15. ___eep ○ pl ○ sl ○ cl	16. ca___ ○ st ○ lt ○ ft
17. sa___ ○ lt ○ st ○ nt	18. ___eet ○ sp ○ sw ○ sn	19. mi___ ○ mp ○ nk ○ sk	20. po___ ○ nk ○ nt ○ st

Sounds of y

That mummy took my YO-YO!

y = y   y = ī

y = ē

1. 🗣 Say each picture name.   2. 👂 Listen for the sound of **y**.
3. ✏️ Find the word in the box and write it on the line.
4. ✏️ Circle the letter that stands for the sound of **y** you hear.

daisy	spy	ferry	yam	fifty	cry	puppy	yard
sky	year	study	dry	yarn	penny	yell	cherry

ⓔ ī y **puppy**	ē ī y	ē ī y	ē ī y
ē ī y	ē ī y	ē ī y	ē ī y
ē ī y	ē ī y	ē ī y	ē ī y
ē ī y	ē ī y	ē ī y	ē ī y

Introducing the sounds of **y**: /ē/, /ī/, /y/

Sounds of **y**

1 📖 Read each sentence.
2 ✏️ Circle the word that makes sense in the sentence.

1. I found ⟨**by** / **my**⟩ book on your desk.

2. Mary told a very **funny** / **carry** joke.

3. Bobby likes to **fry** / **fly** his kite.

4. Please **yet** / **yell** loudly if you need any help.

5. Nancy has to **study** / **story** hard for the test.

6. We had to **spy** / **dry** our wet clothes.

7. In what **yarn** / **year** were you born?

8. You will be late if you do not **hurry** / **furry** .

9. The string is one **yes** / **yard** long.

10. Jimmy let us ride on his **pony** / **penny** .

1 📖 Read the story below.   2 🗣 Say each underlined word.
3 👂 Listen to the sound of **y**.   4 ✏️ Above each word, write **ē**, **ī**, or **y** to show the sound of **y** you hear.

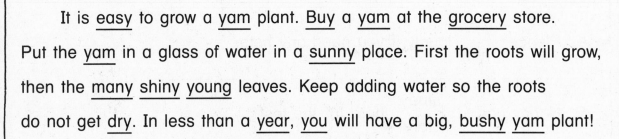

ȳ
Do you know anything about yams? Yams are almost
like sweet potatoes. Yams are orange or red inside.
Sweet potatoes are yellow or white.

Yams are very tasty to eat. Try one next time
you are hungry. You can boil, fry, or bake yams.

It is easy to grow a yam plant. Buy a yam at the grocery store.
Put the yam in a glass of water in a sunny place. First the roots will grow,
then the many shiny young leaves. Keep adding water so the roots
do not get dry. In less than a year, you will have a big, bushy yam plant!

1 📖 Read each question about the story.
2 ✏️ Fill in the space by the correct answer.

1. What is almost like a yam?
   ○ a grocery store
   ● a sweet potato
   ○ a glass of water
   ○ yellow or white

2. Which is one way to cook a yam?
   ○ pry
   ○ try
   ○ fry
   ○ cry

3. What part of a yam plant grows first?
   ○ roots
   ○ leaves
   ○ sunny
   ○ years

4. Which is the best title for this story?
   ○ "Cooking Potatoes"
   ○ "A Year of Work"
   ○ "The Color of a Yam"
   ○ "All About Yams"

Sounds of y

Directions: Read the word in the box. Listen to the sound of **y**. Fill in the space below the word that does **not** have the same sound of **y**.

Example

tiny	lazy	sky	muddy
	○	○	○

1. why	dry ○	lady ○	fry ○	12. berry	jolly ○	try ○	windy ○
2. carry	many ○	by ○	penny ○	13. yam	lazy ○	yoke ○	yap ○
3. you	yarn ○	pony ○	year ○	14. try	why ○	busy ○	dry ○
4. shy	spy ○	sunny ○	fly ○	15. funny	silly ○	carry ○	fly ○
5. hurry	your ○	puppy ○	happy ○	16. yellow	pretty ○	young ○	your ○
6. yes	any ○	yet ○	yell ○	17. my	cry ○	many ○	spy ○
7. very	daisy ○	my ○	body ○	18. hobby	sixty ○	very ○	sky ○
8. by	why ○	shy ○	yak ○	19. your	hurry ○	yes ○	yet ○
9. easy	very ○	crazy ○	cry ○	20. fly	by ○	story ○	try ○
10. yet	tummy ○	yard ○	you ○	21. city	baby ○	study ○	shy ○
11. fry	by ○	daddy ○	my ○	22. yell	every ○	yam ○	you ○

Digraphs: ch, ph, sh, th, wh

"Touch your chin with your thumb three times, and say "cheese"!"

GET in SHIP-SHAPE with SHELLEY

1 Say each picture name. 2 Listen to the first sound.
3 Write the digraph that completes the word.

_sh_ ell	____ale	____eese	____oto	____imble
____eel	____eep	____irty	____imp	____one

1 Read each word.
2 Find the rhyming word in the box and write it on the line.
3 Circle the digraph that stands for the first sound.

| shape   phone   white   thick   chain   while   chance   thank   shut |

nut   (sh)ut   pick _____   cape _____

rain _____   bone _____   pile _____

bite _____   dance _____   rank _____

64

1 📖 Read each sentence.
2 ✏️ Circle the digraph that completes both words in each sentence.
3 ✏️ Write the digraph on the lines.

1. There is a __ch__ ip in the __ch__ ina cup. | (ch) ph sh th wh

2. Bo_____ my friends are in fif_____ grade. | ch ph sh th wh

3. I spent the day fi_____ing at the _____ore. | ch ph sh th wh

4. Do you know _____ere to buy a _____istle? | ch ph sh th wh

5. Phil took a _____oto of the ele_____ant. | ch ph sh th wh

6. I'll wa_____ the di_____es if you'll dry them. | ch ph sh th wh

7. Ea_____ of us wanted to rea_____ the top. | ch ph sh th wh

8. It took a long _____ile to fix the _____eel. | ch ph sh th wh

9. I _____ink there is no_____ing left in the jar. | ch ph sh th wh

10. My ne_____ew called me on the _____one. | ch ph sh th wh

11. The mouse found a _____unk of _____eese. | ch ph sh th wh

12. Do you know _____y snow is _____ite? | ch ph sh th wh

Stretch neck.
2. Swing arms.
3. Catch ring.
4. Check watch.
5. Don't laugh!

ck
ne**ck**

gh
lau**gh**

ng
ri**ng**

tch
wa**tch**

1 Say each picture name.　2 Listen to the last sound.
3 Write the digraph that completes the word.

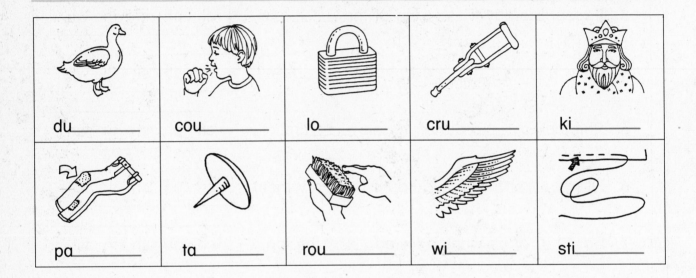

du_____　cou_____　lo_____　cru_____　ki_____

pa_____　ta_____　rou_____　wi_____　sti_____

1 Read each word.
2 Find the rhyming word in the box and write it on the line.
3 Circle the digraph that stands for the last sound.

| ditch | long | block | laugh | lick | fang | tough | batch | fetch |

hang _____　staff _____　smock _____

brick _____　sketch _____　song _____

catch _____　rough _____　itch _____

Introducing consonant digraphs in final position: **ck**; **gh** as /f/; **ng, tch**

1 📖 Read each sentence.
2 ✏️ Circle the digraph that completes both words in each sentence.
3 ✏️ Write the digraph on the lines.

1. Rick put the books ba_____ into his pa_____ .

ck gh ng tch

2. It was funny enou_____ to make me lau_____ .

ck gh ng tch

3. We hu_____ the flag on a lo_____ pole.

ck gh ng tch

4. If you pi_____ the ball, I will ca_____ it.

ck gh ng tch

5. Vicky sat on a ro_____ to eat her sna_____ .

ck gh ng tch

6. My dog Mitch stopped to scra_____ an i_____ .

ck gh ng tch

7. Fixing a rou_____ road is a tou_____ job.

ck gh ng tch

8. The ki_____ wore a ri_____ on his finger.

ck gh ng tch

9. The bla_____ cat crossed the train tra_____ .

ck gh ng tch

10. Ana will sti_____ the pa_____ on the slacks.

ck gh ng tch

11. Did you hear the ti_____ of the clo_____ ?

ck gh ng tch

12. Use some stri_____ to ha_____ the picture.

ck gh ng tch

Using language arts; using sentence context to complete words
with final consonant digraphs: **ck; gh** as /f/; **ng, tch**

67

1 📖 Read each silly question.

2 ✏️ Write **yes** or **no** to answer the question.

1. Can you teach a rock to sing? _no_

4. Can a trophy talk on the phone? _____

2. Can you watch a whale swim by? _____

5. Can you do math in the bath? _____

3. Can a dish have a bad cough? _____

6. Can a chick hatch from a shell? _____

1 📖 Read the words in the box.

2 ✏️ Use words from the box and your own words to write some more silly questions.

chin	fish	truth	why	laugh	can	pick	will
catch	with	song	photo	think	wheel	duck	match
chimp	shop	rough	quack	the	where	stretch	trick
sting	thing	wish	chew	elephant	rich	strong	kick

1. Can a chimp quack? _____

2. _____

3. _____

4. _____

5. _____

Silent Consonants: kn, sc, wr

...knee lifts, scissor kicks, wrist circles!

The letter **k** can be silent when followed by **n**. The letter **w** can be silent when followed by **r**. The letter **c** can be silent when it follows **s**.

kn   wr   sc

knee = k̸nee   **wr**ist = w̸rist   **sc**issors = sc̸issors

---

1. Say each picture name.   2. Listen to the first sound.
3. Write the letters that complete the word.

____ot	____ench	____ientist	____eck	____ob
____ite	____ife	____ap	____enery	____it

---

1. Read each word.
2. Find the rhyming word in the box and write it on the line.
3. Draw a line through the silent consonant in the first sound.

| scene | knock | knit | wrong | kneel | wrote | scent | wring | wrap |

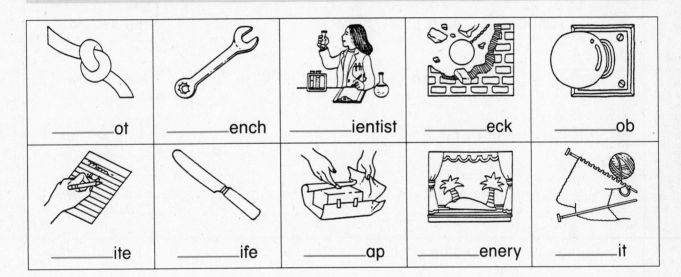

song ___w̸rong___   went _____   bean _____

heel _____   king _____   sit _____

cap _____   rock _____   vote _____

1 📖 Read each sentence.
2 ✏️ Circle the letters that complete the word in each sentence.
3 ✏️ Write the letters on the line.

1. Dan _____ew the answer to the question. | kn sc wr

2. The first _____ene of the play was the best. | kn sc wr

3. The writer _____ote a short story. | kn sc wr

4. Please _____ock before you open the door. | kn sc wr

5. It is _____ong to tell a lie. | kn sc wr

6. We learned about animals in _____ience class. | kn sc wr

7. James wears a watch on his _____ist. | kn sc wr

8. Sally untied the _____ots in the rope. | kn sc wr

9. The sweet _____ent of roses was in the air. | kn sc wr

10. Al used a _____ench to turn the screw. | kn sc wr

11. The house was a _____eck after the party. | kn sc wr

12. My aunt _____it a warm winter hat. | kn sc wr

70

Silent Consonants: dg, gh, mb

You be the judge. Can I climb into these slightly tight tights?

The letter **d** can be silent when followed by **g**. The letter **b** can be silent when it follows **m**. The letters **gh** together can be silent, especially when followed by **t**.

 dg   mb    gh

ju**dge** = ju~~d~~ge   cli**mb** = clim~~b~~   ti**gh**t = ti~~gh~~t

---

1 Say each picture name.
2 Write the letters that complete the word.

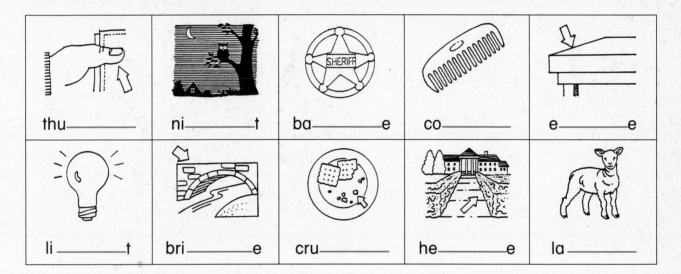

thu_____	ni_____t	ba_____e	co_____	e_____e
li_____t	bri_____e	cru_____	he_____e	la_____

---

1 Read each word.
2 Find the rhyming word in the box and write it on the line.
3 Draw a line through the silent consonant or consonants.

| caught   dumb   limb   lodge   comb   ridge   nudge   fight   right |

taught ___caug~~h~~t___   dodge _____   bite _____

kite _____   budge _____   dim _____

home _____   sum _____   bridge _____

Introducing silent consonants: **dg, gh, mb**

1 📖 Read each sentence.
2 ✏️ Circle the letters that complete the word in each sentence.
3 ✏️ Write the letters on the line.

1. How fast can you cli_____ to the top of the hill? | dg gh mb

2. Patty sits on the ri_____t side of the room. | dg gh mb

3. The officer wore a silver ba_____e on her shirt. | dg gh mb

4. Those new shoes have a bri_____t shine! | dg gh mb

5. This glove has some holes in the thu_____. | dg gh mb

6. The ju_____e told the man to tell the truth. | dg gh mb

7. We mi_____t go to the movies tonight. | dg gh mb

8. Our family stayed at a lo_____e by the lake. | dg gh mb

9. My si_____t is better when I wear my glasses. | dg gh mb

10. The birds did not leave one cru_____ of bread. | dg gh mb

11. There is a large bee on the window le_____e. | dg gh mb

12. Marge can't find her brush and co_____. | dg gh mb

Reviewing
Silent Consonants

1 📖 Read each silly question.
2 ✏️ Write **yes** or **no** to answer the question.

1. Can a lamb comb
   its curls? _____

2. Does a bridge know
   how to write? _____

3. Can there be moonlight
   at night? _____

4. Does a scientist study
   living things? _____

5. Does a wrench have
   two knees? _____

6. Does a judge decide
   what's right or wrong? _____

1 📖 Read the words in the box.
2 ✏️ Use words from the box and your own words to write
some more silly questions.

climb	might	wrist	know	can	scene	the	badge
thumb	wreck	does	tight	knee	edge	wrap	scent
knob	crumb	write	bright	wrong	will	dodge	sight
lamb	wrench	knot	science	bridge	knock	wedge	knit

1. _____

2. _____

3. _____

4. _____

5. _____

1 📖 Read each sentence.
2 ✏️ Circle the letters that complete both words in each sentence.
3 ✏️ Write the letters on the lines.

1. Did you _____ock before turning the _____ob?

| wh | ck | kn | ng |

2. The ju_____e gave the officer a ba _____e.

| ph | dg | sc | mb |

3. We have to wa _____ the white _____eets.

| sh | th | wr | tch |

4. I need a pa_____ that will ma _____ my pants.

| gh | ck | tch | kn |

5. Whi_____ shell did you find on the bea _____?

| wh | sc | th | ch |

6. Drive the tru _____ around the blo _____.

| ph | ck | ng | mb |

7. Beth _____ote down the _____ong number.

| sh | sc | wr | tch |

8. Ruth _____anked me for the bir _____day gift.

| kn | wh | dg | th |

9. Phil saw a bri _____t light in the ni _____t sky.

| gh | ck | sh | mb |

10. Ann hu _____ up when the doorbell ra _____.

| tch | ng | dg | wr |

11. There is a mad _____ientist in that _____ene.

| kn | th | sc | wh |

12. We have to cli _____ to the highest li _____.

| mb | ck | ph | sh |

Unit review: using sentence context to complete words with consonant digraphs or silent consonants

Digraphs and Silent Consonants

Directions: Fill in the space next to the letters that will complete the word.

Example

___ot

○ ng
○ kn
○ th

---

1. ___est

○ ch
○ mb
○ th

2. sa___

○ sc
○ ph
○ ng

3. wi___

○ sh
○ kn
○ wh

4. lau___

○ gh
○ dg
○ th

5. ma___

○ wr
○ tch
○ ph

6. ___one

○ ng
○ ph
○ ck

7. ___ink

○ mb
○ ck
○ th

8. ri___t

○ sc
○ gh
○ ng

9. thu___

○ ch
○ wh
○ mb

10. ___ile

○ sh
○ ng
○ wh

11. che___

○ ck
○ tch
○ sc

12. ___ife

○ mb
○ kn
○ th

13. ___ience

○ gh
○ sc
○ wr

14. do___e

○ sh
○ dg
○ th

15. ___ote

○ ng
○ ck
○ wr

16. ri___

○ gh
○ ch
○ ph

17. ___eep

○ sh
○ ck
○ kn

18. tee___

○ dg
○ wh
○ th

19. gra___

○ ng
○ ph
○ kn

20. ba___

○ wr
○ ck
○ wh

Vowels with **r**: **ar** and **or**

Fishing is such a nice sport!

sha**rk**   sp**or**t

---

1 📖 Read each word.   **2** ✏️ Circle the letters **ar** or **or**.
3 ✏️ Write the letters on the line to complete the word.

1. j(ar)   st_ar_   5. b o r n   t____ch

2. s h o r t   h____n   6. p o r c h   st____m

3. p a r k   b____n   7. s m a r t   c____d

4. y a r d   ch____m   8. c o r n   th____n

---

1 🗣️ Say each picture name.
2 👂 Listen for the sound of **ar** or **or**.
3 ✏️ Find the word above and write it on the line.

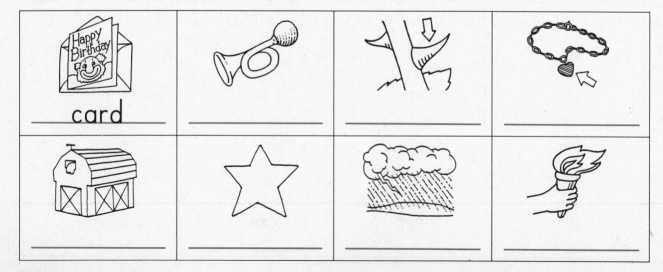

card   ____   ____   ____

____   ____   ____   ____

Introducing r-controlled vowels: **ar**, **or**

1 📖 Read each sentence.
2 ✏️ Circle the word that makes sense in the sentence.
3 ✏️ Write that word on the line.

1. The baby horse was ⎯⎯ born ⎯⎯ late at night.

   barn (born) bore

2. I like to lie on the grass in the ⎯⎯⎯⎯⎯⎯ .

   park   part   pork

3. Do you have a deck of playing ⎯⎯⎯⎯⎯⎯ ?

   cords   cars   cards

4. The cook made ⎯⎯⎯⎯⎯⎯ with apples and cherries.

   tarts   torts   tarps

5. Dad sits on the front ⎯⎯⎯⎯⎯⎯ and reads.

   parch   porch   pores

6. Mom had to use ⎯⎯⎯⎯⎯⎯ to open the window.

   farce   force   ford

7. A ⎯⎯⎯⎯⎯⎯ is a large bird with a long neck.

   stark   store   stork

8. Sue has a ⎯⎯⎯⎯⎯⎯ in the school play.

   poor   part   port

9. Many kinds of crops are grown on this ⎯⎯⎯⎯⎯⎯ .

   farm   form   far

Vowels with r:
ear, er, ir, ur

The letters **ear**, **er**, **ir**, and **ur** can stand for the same sound.

Does the rarest bird on earth have fur and sit on a perch?

earth

perch

bird

fur

---

1 📖 Read each word. **2** ✏️ Circle the letters **ear**, **er**, **ir**, or **ur**.
3 ✏️ Write the letters on the line to complete the word.

1. d i r t   st_____

2. c l e r k   f_____n

3. c u r b   n_____se

4. e a r l y   p_____l

5. h u r t   b_____st

6. l e a r n   s_____ch

7. g i r l   sk_____t

8. s e r v e   h_____d

---

1 🗣️ Say each picture name.
2 👂 Listen for the sound of **ear**, **er**, **ir**, or **ur**.
3 ✏️ Find the word above and write it on the line.

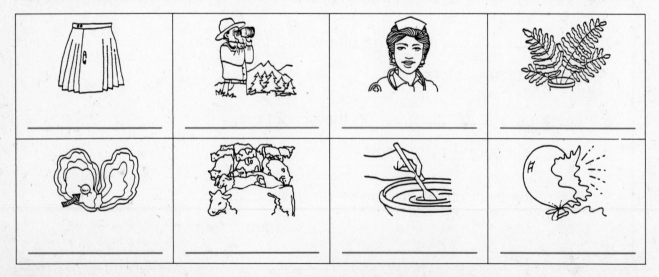

Introducing **r**-controlled vowels: **ear**, **er**, **ir**, **ur** as /èr/

1 📖 Read each sentence.
2 ✏️ Circle the word that makes sense in the sentence.
3 ✏️ Write that word on the line.

1. The waiter will _____ us the dinner.

   search   serve   skirt

2. Park your car close to that _____.

   curb   curl   card

3. The _____ is the third planet from the sun.

   early   earn   earth

4. Please _____ that soup with this spoon.

   short   stir   shirt

5. I always work harder at the end of the school _____.

   torn   turn   term

6. Is this the _____ time you have been here?

   fern   first   firm

7. Burt will _____ the wood to make a fire.

   bird   burst   burn

8. Mom has a necklace made of white _____.

   pearls   purses   perches

9. Our birds _____ when they are happy.

   chore   churn   chirp

Vowels with **r**: air, are, ear

The letters **air** and **are** can stand for the sound you hear in **pair**.

The letters **ear** can stand for the sound you hear in **pair** and the sound you hear in **ear**.

p**air**   squ**are**   b**ear**   **ear**

| 📖 Read each word. | 2 ✏️ Circle the letters **air**, **are**, or **ear**. |

3 ✏️ Write the letters on the line to complete the word.

1. w e a r   p_____   5. d e a r   g_____

2. a i r   f_____y   6. s c a r e   sh_____

3. n e a r   b_____d   7. f l a i r   ch_____

4. c a r e   m_____   8. s w e a r   b_____

---

1 Say each picture name.
2 Listen for the sound of **air**, **are**, or **ear**.
3 ✏️ Find the word above and write it on the line.

Introducing **r**-controlled vowels: air, are, ear as /âr/; ear as /îr/

1 📖 Read each sentence.
2 ✏️ Circle the word that makes sense in the sentence.
3 ✏️ Write that word on the line.

1. Billy will _____ his popcorn with Marta.

   shear   share   stare

2. It is only _____ to wait your turn in line.

   fair   fear   flair

3. Apples and _____ are good fruits to eat.

   pearls   pears   purrs

4. Can you _____ the telephone ringing?

   hair   harm   hear

5. In one more _____, Betsy will be ten.

   yarn   year   yearn

6. The _____ slept inside the log all winter.

   bear   barn   blare

7. We climbed the _____ to the second floor.

   steers   starts   stairs

8. Tess did not _____ to talk during the test.

   dear   dare   dart

9. The sky was _____ after the storm.

   clay   car   clear

1 📖 Read the words in the box. 2 📖 Read each clue.
3 ✏️ Write the correct word in the puzzle.

heard	park
dirt	serve
purple	fare
curb	harbor
beard	oranges
burn	rare
stairs	Thursday
bear	corner
art	target
birthday	

ACROSS

5. Painting and drawing
6. To set on fire
7. Fruit with sweet juice
9. Place with benches and trees
10. Loose earth or soil
11. Day you were born
13. Good port for ships
15. To place food on a table
16. Hair on a man's face
17. Not cooked very much

DOWN

1. Side of a road
2. Place where two walls meet
3. Day after Wednesday
4. A mark you aim at
8. Steps between floors
9. Made by mixing red and blue
12. The cost of a bus ride
13. Listened to
14. A large, furry animal

Vowels with **r**

Directions: Say each picture name.
Listen to the vowel sound. Fill in the
space next to the word that does **not** have
the same vowel sound as the picture name.

Example

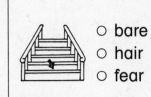

- ○ bare
- ○ hair
- ○ fear

1.
- ○ far
- ○ mark
- ○ pair

2.
- ○ bare
- ○ bark
- ○ chair

3.
- ○ smart
- ○ share
- ○ bear

4.
- ○ sport
- ○ fort
- ○ farm

5.
- ○ her
- ○ burst
- ○ port

6.
- ○ dirt
- ○ curve
- ○ score

7.
- ○ march
- ○ birth
- ○ early

8.
- ○ hair
- ○ shark
- ○ glare

9.
- ○ rare
- ○ arm
- ○ card

10.
- ○ hear
- ○ dear
- ○ hard

11.
- ○ germ
- ○ cork
- ○ horse

12.
- ○ curl
- ○ earn
- ○ part

13.
- ○ fair
- ○ chart
- ○ care

14.
- ○ worn
- ○ learn
- ○ nurse

15.
- ○ stair
- ○ scar
- ○ dare

16.
- ○ dark
- ○ air
- ○ wear

17.
- ○ girl
- ○ born
- ○ fur

18.
- ○ clear
- ○ clerk
- ○ first

19.
- ○ yarn
- ○ year
- ○ fear

20.
- ○ third
- ○ hare
- ○ serve

Testing **r**-controlled vowels; using an adapted standardized test format

Vowel Sounds: ew, oo

COOK with BROOK

STEW

The letters **oo** can stand for the sound you hear in **cook** or the sound you hear in **spoon**.

The letters **ew** can stand for the same sound as the letters **oo** in **spoon**.

cook   spoon   stew

1 Say each picture name.
2 Listen for the sounds of **oo** and **ew**.
3 Find the word in the box and write it on the line.
4 Circle the words that have the vowel sound you hear in **spoon**.

hook	rooster	broom	grew	tooth	news
screw	book	zoo	chew	hood	foot

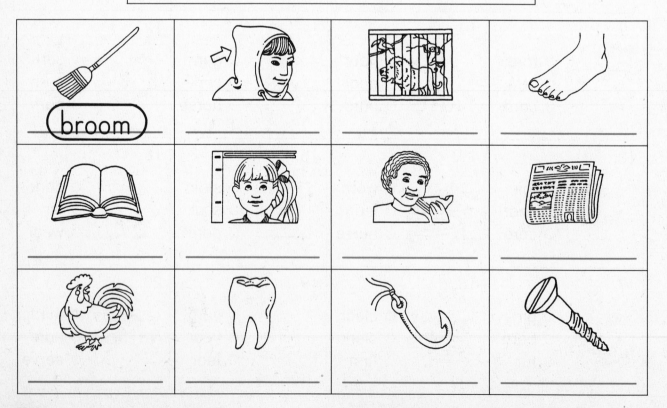

broom

_____   _____   _____   _____

_____   _____   _____   _____

_____   _____   _____   _____

84

1 📖 Read each sentence.   2 🤚 Say the picture name.
3 ✏️ Circle the word that makes sense in the sentence and has the same vowel sound as the picture name.   4 ✏️ Write it on the line.

1. Mary always _____ cooks _____ her food well.

   chews   (cooks)   hoofs

2. Jud _____ the football to his friend.

   threw   knew   took

3. Let's go for a swim in the _____ .

   pew   brook   pool

4. Did you read the _____ about the fire?

   book   news   good

5. My _____ hurt, so I went to a doctor.

   foot   few   tooth

6. Ellen put the _____ into the wood.

   hook   screw   room

7. Bob _____ a picture of a caboose.

   flew   drew   took

8. We saw a raccoon on our trip to the _____ .

   zoo   woods   crew

9. The wind _____ the leaves off the tree.

   shook   noon   blew

Enough bread!

The letters **ea** can stand for the short sound of **e** you hear in **bread**.

The letters **ou** can stand for the short sound of **u** you hear in **enough**.

br**ea**d   en**ou**gh

1 🗣 Say each picture name.
2 👂 Listen for the short sounds of **ea** and **ou**.
3 ✏️ Find the word in the box and write it on the line.
4 ✏️ Circle the words that have the vowel sound you hear in **bread**.

head	double	leather	sweat	couple	rough
thread	touch	heavy	famous	feather	sweater

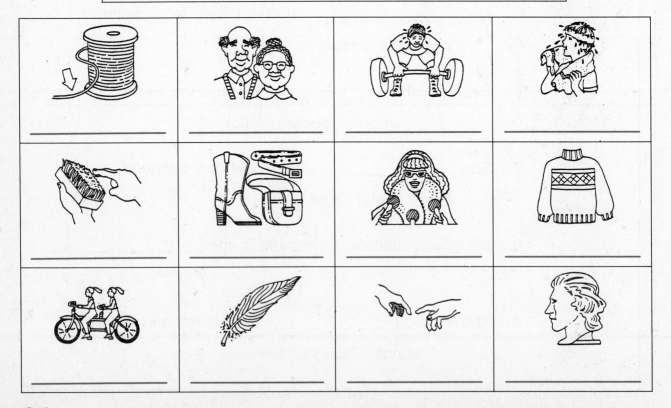

1 📖 Read each sentence.   2 ✏ Say the picture name.
3 ✏ Circle the word that makes sense in the sentence and has
the same vowel sound as the picture name.   4 ✏ Write it on the line.

1. The wool blanket was _____ and scratchy.

   heavy   country   rough

2. Our team will be _____ soon.

   ahead   famous   meant

3. Stan drew a _____ line on his paper.

   red   trouble   double

4. Lynn _____ the wall with a ruler.

   measured   breath   touched

5. I saw that _____ in the store today.

   couple   sweater   sent

6. Digging a hole is a _____ job.

   pleasant   hunt   tough

7. The _____ is hot and dry in the summer.

   country   wet   weather

8. A lamb is a _____ sheep.

   baby   trouble   young

9. I have seen _____ progress in your work.

   spread   enough   steady

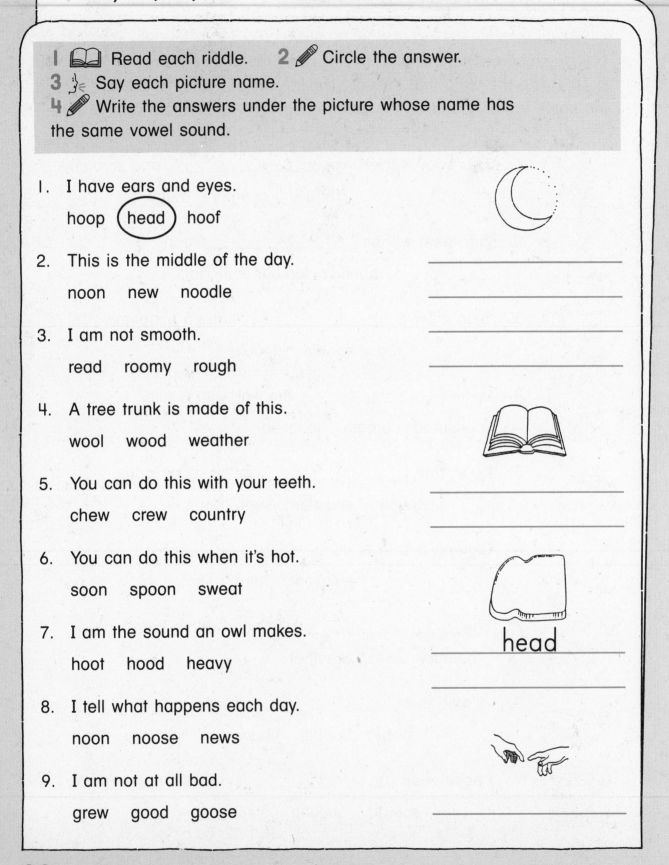

1 📖 Read each riddle.   2 ✏️ Circle the answer.
3 🗣 Say each picture name.
4 ✏️ Write the answers under the picture whose name has
the same vowel sound.

1. I have ears and eyes.
    hoop (head) hoof

2. This is the middle of the day.
    noon   new   noodle

3. I am not smooth.
    read   roomy   rough

4. A tree trunk is made of this.
    wool   wood   weather

5. You can do this with your teeth.
    chew   crew   country

6. You can do this when it's hot.
    soon   spoon   sweat

7. I am the sound an owl makes.
    hoot   hood   heavy

8. I tell what happens each day.
    noon   noose   news

9. I am not at all bad.
    grew   good   goose

head

Reviewing vowel digraphs; using context clues to identify and write words with vowel digraphs

Vowel Sounds: al, all, au, aw

A pinch of salt in the sauce...

Awful!

The letters **au** and **aw** can stand for the same sound.

The letter **a** when followed by **l** or **ll** can stand for the same sound as the letters **au** and **aw**.

s**au**ce   s**aw**   s**al**t   b**all**

---

1 🗣 Say each picture name.

2 👂 Listen for the vowel sound you hear in **saw**.

3 ✏️ Find the word in the box and write it on the line.

fall	yawn	bald	draw	auto	mall
jaw	caught	straw	walrus	faucet	paw

Introducing spelling patterns for /ô/: a(l), a(ll), au, aw

1 📖 Read each sentence.   2 Say the picture name.
3 ✏️ Circle the word that makes sense in the sentence and has the same vowel sound as the picture name.   4 ✏️ Write it on the line.

1. Mom washed the dirty _____ in the sink.

    glasses   laundry   yawns

2. Sam sat on the _____ in front of his house.

    lawn   grass   caught

3. The _____ puppy was very cute.

    fat   salt   small

4. My birthday is in the month of _____ .

    August   May   June

5. In art class we always _____ pictures.

    auto   draw   paint

6. Lisa _____ her new kitten "Fluffy."

    fault   calls   named

7. Did you know the water _____ is leaking?

    faucet   tank   because

8. The ice on the lake began to _____ .

    crack   sauce   thaw

9. Our team lines up next to the _____ .

    wall   false   rail

90

Vowel Sounds: ea, ei

The letters **ea** and **ei** can stand for the long sound of **a**.

st**ea**k

w**ei**gh

1 🗣 Say each picture name.
2 👂 Listen for the long sound of **a**.
3 ✏️ Find the word in the box and write it on the line.

great	reindeer	veil	eighty	freight	reins
sleigh	neighbor	vein	steak	break	lei

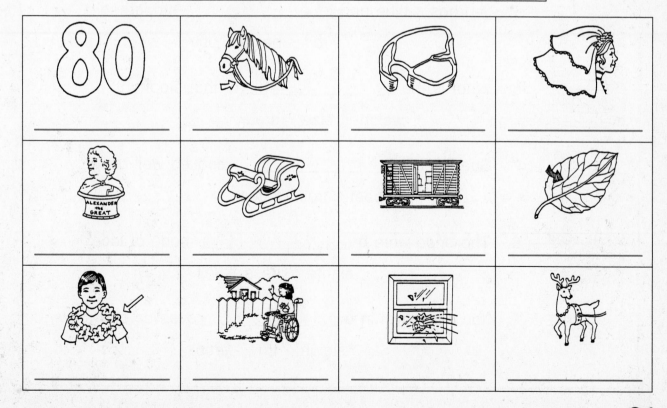

Vowel Sounds: ea, ei

_____

1 📖 Read each sentence.   2 🗣 Say the picture name.
3 ✏️ Circle the word that makes sense in the sentence and has
the same vowel sound as the picture name.   4 ✏️ Write it on the line.

1. The girl took a short _____ from her work.

    rest   break   reins

2. Dave goes to bed at _____ o'clock.

    tame   eight   ten

3. My _____ across the street has a dog.

    neighbor   friend   freight

4. We saw a really _____ movie last night.

    scary   grain   great

5. Jed has a blue and _____ striped shirt.

    red   beige   bay

6. What is the _____ of that elephant?

    weight   size   break

7. Sue likes her _____ cooked well done.

    beef   train   steak

8. The bride wore a _____ made of lace.

    eighty   dress   veil

9. You can travel in a _____ over ice and snow.

    sleigh   tray   jeep

92

1 📖 Read each riddle. 2 ✏️ Circle the answer.
3 ✋ Say each picture name.
4 ✏️ Write the answers under the picture whose name has the same vowel sound.

1. I can travel down the highway.

   August   awning   auto

2. I am a juicy slice of meat.

   steak   small   sleigh

3. I am the sound that a horse makes.

   naughty   neigh   neighbor

4. I am the foot of a dog or a cat.

   paw   pause   pawn

5. I am a head without any hair.

   ball   because   bald

6. I am a necklace made of flowers.

   law   lei   laundry

7. I can be poured over food.

   sauce   saw   stall

8. I can do what the sun can do to ice.

   taught   tall   thaw

9. I am what is not true.

   freight   false   fall

Reviewing spelling patterns for /ô/ and vowel digraphs; using context clues
to identify and write words with spelling patterns for /ô/ and vowel digraphs

93

Vowel Sounds: igh, ind

Just right!

The letters **igh** can stand for the long sound of **i** you hear in **knight**.

The letter **i** when followed by **nd** can stand for the long sound of **i** you hear in **rind**.

kn**igh**t   r**ind**

1. Say each picture name.
2. Listen for the long sound of **i**.
3. Find the word in the box and write it on the line.

wind	tight	highway	blind	light	behind
flight	hind	midnight	grind	thigh	find

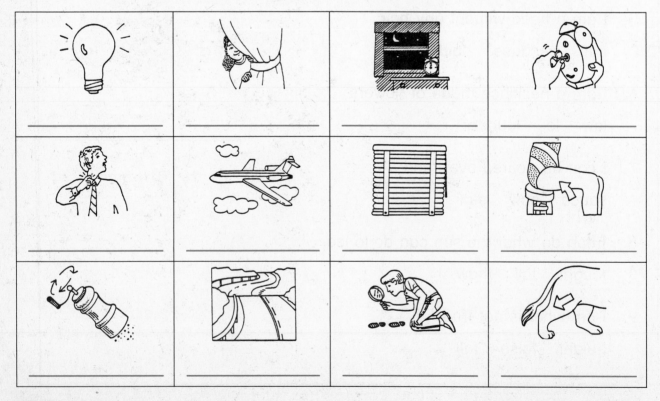

94

Introducing variant spelling patterns for /ī/: **igh, i(nd)**

1 📖 Read each sentence. 2 Say the picture name.
3 ✏️ Circle the word that makes sense in the sentence and has the same vowel sound as the picture name. 4 ✏️ Write it on the line.

1. Dave sold his bike for a _____ price.

    low   high   wind

2. Can you see _____ that brick wall?

    behind   remind   over

3. Your _____ is part of your leg.

    knee   thigh   mind

4. Dad asked the butcher to _____ the meat.

    night   chop   grind

5. What is the _____ way to bind a book?

    right   might   best

6. You must always be _____ to animals.

    gentle   kind   sigh

7. Our _____ will take off soon.

    plane   blind   flight

8. The horse hurt one of its _____ legs.

    hind   sight   front

9. Where did you _____ those purple shoes?

    fight   find   get

Vowel Sounds:
old, oll, olt, ow

COLD
SNOW
ROLLS

The letters **ow** can stand for the long sound of **o**.

The letter **o** when followed by **ld**, **ll**, or **lt** can stand for the long sound of **o** you hear in **cold**, **roll**, and **bolt**.

sn**ow**   c**old**   r**oll**   b**olt**

1 🗣 Say each picture name.
2 👂 Listen for the long sound of **o**.
3 ✏️ Find the word in the box and write it on the line.

gold	scroll	tow	fold	blow	throw
sold	colt	toll	crow	row	mow

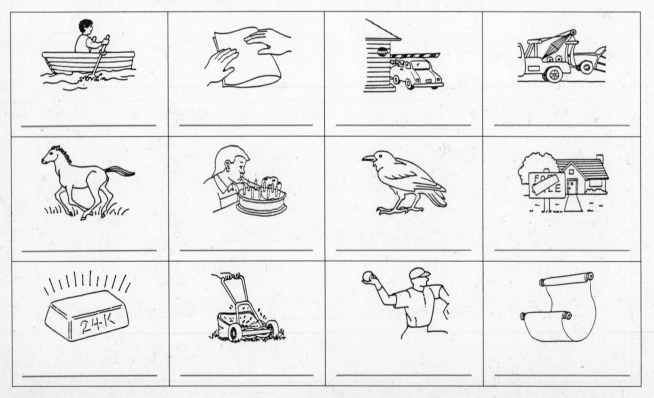

96

1 📖 Read each sentence.   2 👆 Say the picture name.
3 ✏️ Circle the word that makes sense in the sentence and has
the same vowel sound as the picture name.   4 ✏️ Write it on the line.

1. Patty sat down in the last _____ .

  seat   row   crow

2. Our car will only _____ six people.

  carry   bolt   hold

3. You must pay a _____ to cross the bridge.

  toll   dime   fold

4. Mrs. Sam _____ that large house.

  owns   blown   cleans

5. Steve _____ me about his new school.

  called   told   stroll

6. Have you ever tried to _____ seeds?

  flow   plant   grow

7. Mike spread butter on the _____ .

  roll   old   bread

8. Will you _____ me how to tie a knot?

  bowl   show   teach

9. The small _____ slept in the barn.

  colt   lamb   bold

Using language arts; using sentence context to select words
with variant spelling patterns for /ō/: o(ld), o(ll), o(lt), ow

97

Vowel Sounds: ey, ie

The letters **ey** and **ie** can stand for the long sound of **e**.

hon**ey**   th**ie**f

1. 🗣 Say each picture name.
2. 👂 Listen for the long sound of **e**.
3. ✏️ Find the word in the box and write it on the line.

valley	chief	monkey	key	movie	donkey
shield	alley	chimney	collie	money	field

Vowel Sounds: ey, ie

1 📖 Read each sentence.   2 🗣 Say the picture name.
3 ✏️ Circle the word that makes sense in the sentence and has the same vowel sound as the picture name.   4 ✏️ Write it on the line.

1. The baseball players are on the _____ .

   bench   field   brief

2. Pennies and dimes are kinds of _____ .

   money   honey   coins

3. Mom had to make a _____ stop at the store.

   short   leaf   brief

4. There is a dark _____ between those buildings.

   alley   tasty   path

5. Frank's new puppy is a _____ .

   mutt   tree   collie

6. Did you see the smoke from the _____ ?

   parsley   chimney   fire

7. They live in a _____ between two mountains.

   village   funny   valley

8. Jan wrote a note to her _____ .

   neighbor   neat   niece

9. Can you cut a big _____ of cheese?

   slice   peach   piece

Reviewing Vowel Sounds:
**ey, ie, igh, ind,
old, oll, olt, ow**

_____

1 📖 Read each riddle. 2 ✏️ Circle the answer.
3 🗣 Say each picture name.
4 ✏️ Write the answers under the picture whose name has
the same vowel sound.

1. I can open a locked door.

   know   key   knoll

2. I am very brave.

   believe   bold   bolt

   _____
   _____

3. I am a large, black bird.

   crow   colt   chief

4. I cannot see with my eyes.

   bowl   blind   brief

   _____
   _____

5. I can be seen on a big screen.

   mold   mow   movie

   _____
   _____

6. I can be used to make rings.

   gold   grief   grow

   _____

7. I can be found in fairy tales.

   toll   told   troll

8. I am not loose.

   told   throw   tight

   _____
   _____

9. I have soft, white flakes.

   sold   snow   shield

Reviewing variant spelling patterns and vowel digraphs; using context clues
to identify and write words with variant spelling patterns and vowel digraphs

Vowel Sounds: ou, ow

The letters **ou** can stand for the sound you hear in **mouse**.

The letters **ow** can stand for the same sound as the letters **ou** in **mouse**.

m**ou**se   c**ow**

1 🗣 Say each picture name.
2 👂 Listen for the sound of **ou** and **ow**.
3 ✏️ Find the word in the box and write it on the line.

| town | spout | house | bounce | plow | cloud |
| clown | blouse | towel | pouch | owl | crown |

_____   _____   _____   _____

_____   _____   _____   _____

_____   _____   _____   _____

Vowel Sounds: ou, ow

1 📖 Read each sentence.   2 ✌ Say the picture name.
3 ✏ Circle the word that makes sense in the sentence and has
the same vowel sound as the picture name.   4 ✏ Write it on the line.

1. The leaves of the tree turn _____ in fall.

    red   brown   count

2. How many _____ does a whale weigh?

    frowns   pounds   tons

3. Jack wiped the sweat off his _____ .

    brow   face   found

4. Joan walked _____ the steep stairs.

    clown   up   down

5. We heard the dog _____ late last night.

    bark   howl   sprout

6. The town is five miles _____ of here.

    vowel   west   south

7. There isn't a _____ in the sky!

    star   now   cloud

8. Please _____ so I can hear you.

    shout   yell   towel

9. Sally put the _____ in a vase.

    roses   showers   flowers

Using language arts; using sentence context to select words with vowel diphthongs: **ou**, **ow** as /ou/

Vowel Sounds: **oi, oy**

Boil the oysters.

The letters **oi** and **oy** can stand for the same sound.

b**oi**l   **oy**ster

1. Say each picture name.
2. Listen for the sound of **oi** and **oy**.
3. Find the word in the box and write it on the line.

noise	foil	point	toy	royal	joy
coin	oil	boy	voice	oink	broil

1 📖 Read each sentence.   2 🗣 Say the picture name.
3 ✏️ Circle the word that makes sense in the sentence and has
the same vowel sound as the picture name.   4 ✏️ Write it on the line.

1. Joy fried the eggs in _____ .

toy   oil   grease

2. Is that _____ a friend of yours?

boy   boil   man

3. Listen to that loud _____ .

coil   crash   noise

4. The little girl played with her _____ .

doll   toy   toil

5. Our team is winning by six _____ .

points   moist   runs

6. We found _____ shells on the shore.

clam   voice   oyster

7. Roy has to _____ these parts together.

joy   join   glue

8. The meat will _____ in the hot sun.

spoil   rot   royal

9. Did you _____ the cowboy movie?

like   loyal   enjoy

Using language arts; using sentence context to select words with vowel diphthongs: **oi, oy** as /oi/

1 📖 Read each riddle. 2 ✏️ Circle the answer.
3 🗣 Say each picture name.
4 ✏️ Write the answers under the picture whose name has
the same vowel sound.

1. I can make you laugh.

   cloud   clown   cold

2. I am found in sea water.

   show   sight   salt

3. I am a very happy feeling.

   joy   jewel   join

4. You can use this to sweep.

   beige   broom   bind

5. These are people who work on a plane.

   crew   crow   crawl

6. You can pour water out of this.

   stroll   spoil   spout

7. I am a rocket blastoff.

   loop   launch   law

8. You can find this on the foot of an animal.

   chief   claw   cool

9. I am a way to cook a steak.

   brook   breath   broil

Unit review: using context clues to identify and write words
with variant spelling patterns, vowel digraphs and diphthongs

105

1 📖 Read the words.

2 ✏️ Make a sentence by writing the words in the right order.

1. over hawk house. flew A our

   A hawk flew over our house.

2. troop. cousin to belongs My scout a

   _____

3. a scolded boy. chief The naughty

   _____

4. kick their Donkeys legs. with hind

   _____

5. head. man The his old shook bald

   _____

6. in I ride a snow. sleigh the enjoy

   _____

7. you that Did noise? loud hear

   _____

8. field. stood the in Cows

   _____

9. need light a We alley. in bright the

   _____

Unit review: writing sentences with words with variant spelling patterns, vowel digraphs and diphthongs

1 📖 Read each verse.
2 ✏️ Complete the verse by finding a rhyming word in the box and writing it on the line.

eight   moon   cook   dawn

1. Under the _____moon_____ ,

   The wolf howled a tune.

2. Do you know a good book

   That tells how to _____ ?

3. There is dew on the lawn

   Just before _____ .

4. If it is _____ ,

   I'm already late!

1 📖 Read the words in the box.   2 🔍 Find pairs of words that rhyme.   3 ✏️ Use those words to write your own verses.

weigh great piece loud plate stuff mind old
tough find sold say crowd grease thief beef

1. Can you please say
   How much you weigh?

2. _____

   _____

3. _____

   _____

4. _____

   _____

Other Vowel Sounds

Directions: Read the words in the box. Listen to the vowel sound. Fill in the space below the word with the same vowel sound as the word in the box.

Example

cow	cool	couch	coil
	○	○	○

1. boot	blew ○	boy ○	bolt ○	12. right	rein ○	rind ○	rig ○
2. weigh	well ○	wind ○	wait ○	13. toy	tough ○	took ○	toil ○
3. mind	moist ○	might ○	mint ○	14. bold	bowl ○	book ○	boil ○
4. touch	tub ○	told ○	toy ○	15. thread	threw ○	test ○	thaw ○
5. colt	cook ○	cow ○	cold ○	16. house	haul ○	hook ○	how ○
6. stood	stop ○	shout ○	shook ○	17. now	noon ○	noun ○	new ○
7. key	knew ○	kept ○	knee ○	18. caught	crawl ○	catch ○	crate ○
8. paw	plow ○	pound ○	pause ○	19. small	sweat ○	snail ○	shawl ○
9. grow	goat ○	good ○	ground ○	20. break	brass ○	beige ○	bald ○
10. chew	chow ○	choose ○	choice ○	21. chief	cheese ○	chain ○	coin ○
11. join	jolt ○	job ○	joy ○	22. stroll	soil ○	sold ○	soon ○

Testing variant spelling patterns, vowel digraphs and diphthongs; using an adapted standardized test format

Compound Words

OH no! A waterfall!

A compound word is a word made up of two smaller words.

water + fall = waterfall

1 ✏️ Draw lines to make compound words.   2 👂 Say each picture name.
3 ✏️ Write the compound word that names the picture.

butter	lace	paint	nail	flash	fruit
neck	fish	row	boat	grape	bell
air	fly	pop	brush	snow	ball
star	port	finger	corn	door	light

starfish

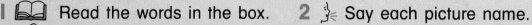

1 Read the words in the box.　2 Say each picture name.
3 Write the two words that make up each picture name.
4 Write the words together to make a compound word.

pot	pan	mill	rain	work	sea	news	sun	foot
shell	bow	bare	cake	wind	tea	set	paper	book

　___sun___ + ___set___ = ___sunset___

　_____ + _____ = _____

　_____ + _____ = _____

　_____ + _____ = _____

　_____ + _____ = _____

　_____ + _____ = _____

　_____ + _____ = _____

　_____ + _____ = _____

_____ + _____ = _____

110

Compound Words

1 📖 Read each question.
2 ✏ Underline the compound word and draw a line between its two smaller words.   3 ✏ Circle the answer.

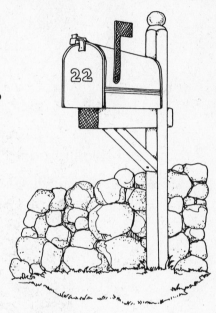

1. What would you find in a mail|box?
   eyelids (postcards) pigtails

2. What would you find in a barnyard?
   pigpen   houseboat   hallway

3. What can you see only at nighttime?
   anyhow   meatloaf   moonlight

4. What can you eat for breakfast?
   pancakes   rainbow   runway

5. What could you find in a backyard?
   nickname   clothesline   cupboard

6. What can you ride on the sidewalk?
   sailboat   toolbox   skateboard

7. What could you find in a lunchbox?
   downtown   popcorn   doghouse

8. What might you find with a schoolbook?
   notebook   nobody   bluebird

9. What could you find at the seashore?
   railroad   starfish   drumstick

Syllables

Escape to the airplane!

A syllable is a word or part of a word that has one vowel sound.

 leaf

1 vowel sound = 1 syllable

 air/plane

2 vowel sounds = 2 syllables

 vol/ca/no

3 vowel sounds = 3 syllables

1　Say each picture name.
2　Listen for the vowel sound or sounds.
3　Write the number of syllables you hear.

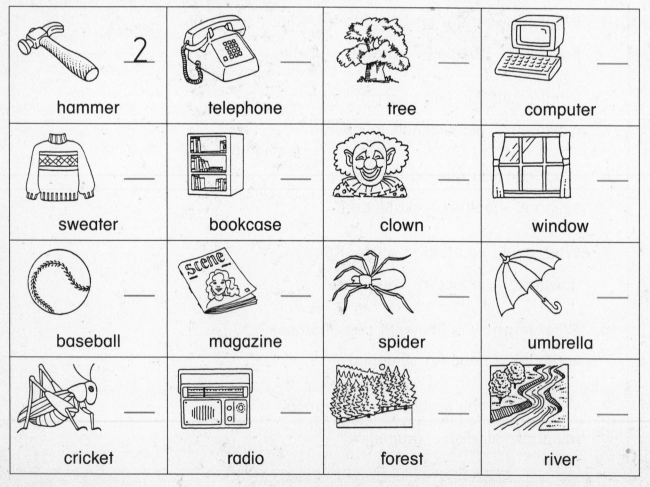

hammer — 2	telephone —	tree —	computer —
sweater —	bookcase —	clown —	window —
baseball —	magazine —	spider —	umbrella —
cricket —	radio —	forest —	river —

Syllables

1 📖 Read each word.   2 ✏️ Underline the vowel or vowels.
3 🗣️ Say the word.   4 👂 Listen for the vowel sound or sounds.
5 ✏️ Write the number of vowels, the number of vowel sounds,
and then the number of syllables.

	Vowels		Number of Syllables		Vowels		Number of Syllables
	seen	heard			seen	heard	
peach	2	1	1	cloud	—	—	—
peacock	—	—	—	Saturday	—	—	—
ladder	—	—	—	school	—	—	—
sideways	—	—	—	afraid	—	—	—
office	—	—	—	become	—	—	—
rain	—	—	—	feather	—	—	—
interest	—	—	—	evening	—	—	—
number	—	—	—	potato	—	—	—
until	—	—	—	doghouse	—	—	—
pointed	—	—	—	quite	—	—	—
rabbit	—	—	—	village	—	—	—
elephant	—	—	—	tomorrow	—	—	—

1 📖 Read each sentence.

2 ✏️ Choose a word from the box that makes sense in the sentence and write it on the line.

supper	library	artist	homework	winter
exercise	together	magic	garbage	detective

1. Steve took out a book from the city _____library_____ .

2. Linda always does her math _____ after school.

3. The _____ was hired to help solve the crime.

4. Jill glued the pieces of wood _____ .

5. Jerry threw the _____ in the trash can.

6. It can be very cold in the _____ .

7. That _____ likes to paint pictures of animals.

8. Swimming and running can be good _____ .

9. For _____ we ate chicken and potatoes.

10. My aunt knows how to do _____ tricks.

Using language arts; using sentence context to select and write words with more than one syllable

Reviewing Compound Words and Syllables

1. ✎ Draw lines to make compound words.
2. 🗣 Say each picture name.
3. ✎ Write the number of syllables you hear.
4. ✎ Write the compound word that names the picture.

grass	ship	gold	berry	sales	house
sun	hopper	straw	fish	card	watch
space	stick	waste	toe	stop	board
candle	flower	tip	basket	green	person

3
grasshopper _____

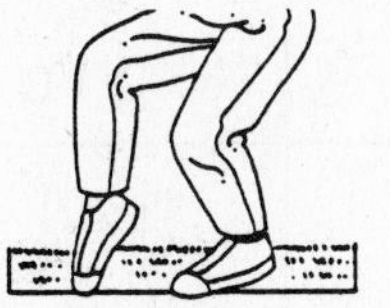

_____

_____

_____

_____

_____

_____

_____

_____

_____

_____

_____

Syllables

Let's unlock all the boxes quickly!

Words are divided into syllables between the prefix or suffix and the base word.

un/lock   **re**/run   quick/**ly**

joy/**ful**   farm/**er**

Words are divided into syllables between some endings and the base word.

count/**ed**   box/**es**   help/**ing**

bright/**est**

1 ✍ Say each picture name.   2 👂 Listen for the prefix, suffix, or ending.

3 ✏️ Write the number of syllables you hear.

4 ✏️ Draw a line between the syllables.

3	___	___	___
un|lo|ad|ed	r e f i l l i n g	c u p f u l	s l o w l y
___	___	___	___
w a i t e r	f a s t e s t	g l a s s e s	c r a c k i n g
___	___	___	___
u n p l u g	r e b u i l d i n g	h e l p f u l	s o f t l y
___	___	___	___
r e p a i n t e d	t e a c h e r	m e l t e d	b u s e s

116

1 📖 Read each word. 2 ✏️ Underline the prefix, suffix, or ending. 3 🗣 Say the word. 4 👂 Listen for the vowel sounds. 5 ✏️ Write the word, leaving a space between the syllables.

small<u>est</u>	small est	recooking	
worker		highest	
dresses		strangely	
remake		roomful	
floated		redoing	
untie		branches	
kisses		unwanted	
hardly		helper	
knocking		swinging	
trailer		closely	
missing		repay	
mouthful		careful	

Using syllables; syllabication of words with affixes

1 📖 Read each sentence.
2 🔍 Choose a word from the box that makes sense in the sentence.
3 ✏️ Write it on the line, leaving a space between the syllables.

youngest	recounted	quickly	sinking	repacking
thankful	rewrite	passes	cooking	player

1. Sandy had to _____ re write _____ the report five times.

2. It was hard to keep my feet from _____ into the mud.

3. The rabbit ran _____ across the field.

4. Karen was _____ for her friend's help.

5. Dad got some free _____ to a magic show.

6. The teacher _____ the children in the room.

7. Kit is _____ her suitcase for the third time.

8. The baseball _____ hit the ball over the fence.

9. My baby sister is the _____ in our family.

10. Do you know what is _____ on the stove?

Using language arts; using sentence context to select words with affixes; syllabication of words with affixes

Syllables

Some words are divided into syllables between the consonants.

din/ner   res/cue

1 🗣 Say each picture name.   2 👂 Listen for the vowel sounds.
3 ✏️ Write the number of syllables you hear.
4 ✏️ Draw a line between the syllables.

3	—	—	—
un|zip|ping	pillow	turkey	strawberry
—	—	—	—
napkin	tennis	puppet	doctor
—	—	—	—
raccoon	gardening	trumpeter	barrelful
—	—	—	—
lettuce	costume	picnic	basketful

Introducing syllables; words with VCCV

Syllables

yellow__ing__   _yel low ing_

picture _____

donkey _____

suppose _____

dinner _____

under _____

happen _____

captain _____

better _____

signaling _____

collect _____

monkey _____

letter _____

funniest _____

dentist _____

rewritten _____

entering _____

dollar _____

silver _____

follow _____

daddy _____

penny _____

window _____

plentiful _____

120

1 📖 Read each sentence.
2 🔍 Choose a word from the box that makes sense in the sentence.
3 ✏️ Write it on the line, leaving a space between the syllables.

| practicing | winner | whisper | hello | sisters |
| hurry | marketing | balloons | pepper | blanketed |

1. The _____ of the race will win a prize.

2. Six inches of new snow _____ the city.

3. Dan added salt and _____ to the stew.

4. Mother said _____ when she answered the phone.

5. We'll be late if you don't _____ .

6. John filled all of the _____ with air.

7. Elena does her _____ on Saturdays.

8. Mary has been _____ the piano for two hours every day.

9. Cliff has two _____ and one brother.

10. Can you _____ the secret in my ear?

1 ✏️ Draw lines to connect the syllables and make words.
2 🗣️ Say each picture name.
3 ✏️ Write the word that names the picture.

re	ed	un	ly	wal	er
thought	move	sad	washed	el	ten
short	est	crutch	ing	mit	bow
land	ful	build	es	catch	let

remove

_____

_____

_____

_____

_____

_____

_____

_____

_____

_____

_____

Reviewing syllables in words with affixes and in words with VCCV

Syllables

Shhh... Tigers surround the Palace.

If the first vowel sound is long, divide the word **before** the next consonant.

 ti/ger

If the first vowel sound is short, divide the word **after** the next consonant.

 pal/ace

---

1 🔈 Say each picture name.   2 👂 Listen carefully to the first vowel sound.
3 ✏️ Write the number of syllables you hear.
4 ✏️ Draw a line between the syllables.

2 ro|bot	___ wagon	___ zebra	___ radishes
___ camel	___ satellite	___ comet	___ computer
___ spider	___ pilot	___ furnishings	___ desert
___ pirate	___ lizard	___ cabin	___ tablecloth

Syllables

lady   lā dy   magic _____

finishing _____   photo _____

stomach _____   pony _____

clever _____   second _____

tiniest _____   never _____

later _____   remodel _____

wonderful _____   body _____

honey _____   shadow _____

notice _____   opening _____

ocean _____   travel _____

visit _____   city _____

broken _____   over _____

Syllables

1 📖 Read each sentence.
2 🔍 Choose a word from the box that makes sense in the sentence.
3 ✏️ Write it on the line, leaving a space between the syllables.

planets	copying	music	dragon	prepare
refrozen	finally	promise	even	seven

1. The story was about a huge, green _____ .

2. Tina is _____ her homework onto a clean sheet of paper.

3. Is six an odd or _____ number?

4. The long, boring play _____ came to an end.

5. Saturn and Venus are names of _____ .

6. Jackson made a _____ to call me.

7. Tomorrow our cooking class will _____ a Chinese meal.

8. Food that has thawed should not be _____ .

9. There are _____ days in a week.

10. What kind of _____ do you like to listen to?

Syllables

Please, don't tickle me!

When a word ends in a consonant followed by **le**, divide the word before the consonant.

jun/**gle**

When a word ends in **ck** followed by **le**, divide the word after **ck**.

tick/**le**

1 Say each picture name. **2** Listen for the vowel sounds.
3 Write the number of syllables you hear.
4 Draw a line between the syllables.

2 tur|tle	triangle	knuckle	castle
cuticle	ladle	juggle	pickle
eagle	beetle	freckle	noodle
bicycle	waffle	tackle	marble

126

Syllables

1 📖 Read each word.   2 ✏️ Underline the consonant plus **le** or **ckle**.
3 🗣 Say the word.   4 👂 Listen for the vowel sounds.
5 ✏️ Write the word, leaving a space between the syllables.

little   _lit tle_____   fickle   _____

circle   _____   dribble   _____

uncle   _____   able   _____

title   _____   fable   _____

cuticle   _____   twinkle   _____

battle   _____   riddle   _____

chuckle   _____   tickle   _____

particle   _____   sizzle   _____

handle   _____   article   _____

simple   _____   pebble   _____

table   _____   people   _____

maple   _____   crackle   _____

Using syllables; syllabication of words ending in Cle

1. 📖 Read each sentence.
2. 🔍 Choose a word from the box that makes sense in the sentence.
3. ✏️ Write it on the line, leaving a space between the syllables.

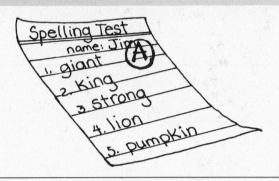

bundle	kettle	tickle	wiggle	simple
buckle	bugle	thimble	gentle	puddle

1. That spelling test was really _____ !

2. Jill always laughs when you _____ her.

3. The _____ on my leather belt is broken.

4. My aunt wears a _____ on her finger when she sews.

5. Put that _____ of newspapers in the basement.

6. George can play taps on his _____ .

7. Ellen walked through a big _____ of water.

8. My father gave the baby a _____ hug.

9. We boiled some water for tea in the _____ .

10. Can you _____ your ears back and forth?

1 ✏️ Draw lines to connect the syllables and make words.
2 🗣️ Say each picture name.
3 ✏️ Write the word that names the picture.

mag	le	sad	u	freck	ble
cra	vy	ba	dle	tum	le
pick	ic	men	kle	ov	ive
gra	dle	wrin	ker	ol	en

Schwa

In an unstressed syllable, the vowels **a**, **e**, **i**, **o**, and **u** can stand for the same sound. This sound is called the schwa sound.

el'/**e**/phant   riv' /**e**r   fos'/s**i**l

par'/r**o**t   cac'/t**u**s

1 Say each picture name.	2 Listen for the schwa sound.

3 Circle the vowel that stands for the schwa sound.

4 Mark the stressed syllable as shown.

cir /c(u)s	um/brel/la	di/ver	pen/cil
cel/lar	al/bum	trac/tor	sal/ad
scis/sors	a/pron	lem/on/ade	ped/al
rul/er	chil/dren	clar/i/net	rib/bon

130

1 📖 Read each word.   2 🗣 Say the word.
3 👂 Listen for the schwa sound.   4 ✏️ Write the word, leaving a
space between the syllables.   5 ✏️ Circle the vowel that stands for
the schwa sound. Mark the syllable that is said with more stress.

a/head	ⓐ head′	ex/tra	
les/son		u/pon	
ov/en		a/long	
fi/nal		care/ful	
ap/ri/cot		a/go	
e/ven		or/der	
a/bout		roos/ter	
oth/er		skel/e/ton	
pa/rade		a/gree	
al/pha/bet		a/cross	
cor/ner		col/or	
a/lone		fal/len	

1 📖 Read each sentence.

2 ✏️ Choose a word from the box that makes sense in the sentence and write it on the line.

possum	camper	dollars	afraid	fingers
buttons	mirror	person	carrot	broken

1. Lee was _____ of the lions at the zoo.

2. Amy tried to fix the chip in the _____ cup.

3. I like to eat a _____ when I'm hungry.

4. We slept in the _____ during our trip.

5. Have you ever seen a movie star in _____?

6. Ed lost one of the _____ on his coat.

7. You have one thumb and four _____ on each hand.

8. The furry _____ hung by its tail from the branch.

9. Five _____ is too much to pay for this notebook.

10. Wally looked at himself in the _____.

132

Using language arts; using sentence context to select and write words with schwa

1 🖊 Draw lines to connect the syllables and make words.
2 🗣 Say each picture name.   3 👂 Listen for the schwa sound.
4 🖊 Write the word that names the picture and then circle the vowel
that stands for the schwa sound.

shov	tern	vo	lon	pen	zel
wal	al	pi	like	pret	cils
med	rus	gal	ter	si	con
lan	el	a	rate	ba	ren

shov(e)l

1 📖 Read each riddle.

2 ✏️ Choose the answer from the box and write it on the line.

stomach	unhappy	castle	pickle	yellow
sweatshirt	umbrella	secret	train	doctor

1. I am a two-syllable word that names
   something you will probably never find out. _____ secret _____

2. I am a compound word that names
   something you can wear when you exercise. _____

3. I am a two-syllable word that names the
   color of a banana. _____

4. I am a three-syllable word that names
   something that keeps you dry in the rain. _____

5. I am a two-syllable word that ends in **le** and
   names a place where a king and queen live. _____

6. I am a one-syllable word that names
   something that travels on a track. _____

7. I am a three-syllable word with a prefix that
   describes being sad. _____

8. I am a two-syllable word that names a part
   of the body. _____

9. I am a two-syllable word that ends in **le** and
   names something you can eat. _____

10. I am a two-syllable word that names
    someone who helps you when you're sick. _____

Unit review: using context clues to identify compound words, syllables, and words with schwa

1 📖 Read each sentence.   2 🎵 Say the picture name.

3 ✏️ Circle the word that makes sense in the sentence and has the same number of syllables as the picture name.

4 ✏️ Write it on the line, leaving a space between the syllables.

1. The _____air plane_____ flew south over the city.

   butterfly (airplane) badly

2. Mother heard the _____ ringing loudly.

   telephone   potato   doorbell

3. When will you _____ the money you owe?

   have   wanted   repay

4. On Sunday we had a _____ lunch at the park.

   wonderful   picnic   pillow

5. This is the _____ time you have been late!

   second   first   salad

6. There is a tiny _____ in the cradle.

   smallest   child   baby

7. Our class stood in a _____ around the flagpole.

   ring   circle   purple

8. My aunt shops at the _____ on the corner.

   store   market   matching

Compound Words, Syllables, and Schwa

Directions: Say each picture name. Listen to the vowel sounds. Fill in the space next to the word that is divided into syllables correctly.

Example

- ○ rob/ot
- ○ r/obot
- ○ ro/bot

1.
- ○ po/pcorn
- ○ pop/corn
- ○ popc/orn

2.
- ○ paint/er
- ○ pa/inter
- ○ pai/nter

3.
- ○ ba/sket
- ○ bas/ket
- ○ baske/t

4.
- ○ pup/pet
- ○ puppe/t
- ○ pu/ppet

5.
- ○ zeb/ra
- ○ ze/bra
- ○ zebr/a

6.
- ○ liz/ard
- ○ li/zard
- ○ liza/rd

7.
- ○ bub/ble
- ○ bubbl/e
- ○ bu/bble

8.
- ○ pic/kle
- ○ pick/le
- ○ pi/ckle

9.
- ○ cac/tus
- ○ cact/us
- ○ ca/ctus

10.
- ○ spo/onful
- ○ spoon/ful
- ○ spoo/nful

11.
- ○ sal/ad
- ○ sa/lad
- ○ sala/d

12.
- ○ ra/inbow
- ○ rain/bow
- ○ rainb/ow

13.
- ○ unlo/ad
- ○ u/nload
- ○ un/load

14.
- ○ ma/tches
- ○ match/es
- ○ matche/s

15.
- ○ turt/le
- ○ tu/rtle
- ○ tur/tle

Testing compound words, syllables, and schwa; using an adapted standardized test format

Contractions: n't

A contraction is made by putting two words together to make one shorter word.

An apostrophe takes the place of the letter or letters that are left out.

did n**o**t → didn't   were n**o**t → weren't

Remember that **won't** stands for **will not**.

---

1 📖 Read the words below.
2 ✏️ Write the contraction that can be made from the words.

hadn't	wasn't	wouldn't	haven't	aren't	don't
doesn't	can't	couldn't	hasn't	isn't	won't

is not _____ isn't _____   has not _____

could not _____   do not _____

was not _____   can not _____

had not _____   have not _____

will not _____   would not _____

are not _____   does not _____

---

1 📖 Read each contraction below.
2 ✏️ Write the two words from which the contraction was made.

haven't ____ have not ____   aren't _____

doesn't _____   don't _____

isn't _____   couldn't _____

won't _____   can't _____

hadn't _____   wasn't _____

Introducing contractions with **n't**

137

1 📖 Read each sentence.
2 ✏️ Write the contraction that completes the sentence.

1. I ____don't____ think I know your name. | don't isn't

2. There _____ any holes in my socks. | won't weren't

3. Tim _____ at school on time today. | wouldn't wasn't

4. Joan _____ let me use her pencil. | won't aren't

5. Our dog _____ stop running away. | wouldn't hadn't

6. They _____ meeting us at the zoo. | hasn't aren't

7. Dan _____ like to do his chores. | doesn't haven't

8. She _____ cross the street alone. | isn't can't

9. Todd _____ forgotten his lunch. | hasn't don't

10. Cesar _____ going to the ball game. | hadn't isn't

11. Why _____ you remember to call? | didn't weren't

12. We _____ finished eating lunch. | haven't shouldn't

138

Contractions:
'm, 's, 're, 've

We're from planet XYZ!

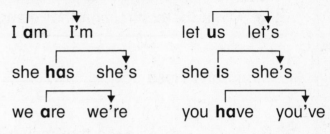

A contraction is made by putting two words together to make one shorter word.

An apostrophe takes the place of the letter or letters that are left out.

I **a**m → I'm   let **us** → let's

she **ha**s → she's   she **is** → she's

we **a**re → we're   you **ha**ve → you've

---

1 📖 Read the words below.

2 ✏️ Write the contraction that can be made from the words.

I'm	he's	I've	who's	they're	that's
let's	it's	we've	you're	they've	what's

that is _____   who is _____

I have _____   I am _____

he has _____   we have _____

you are _____   what is _____

they are _____   it has _____

let us _____   they have _____

---

1 📖 Read each contraction below.

2 ✏️ Write the two words from which the contraction was made.

let's ____let us____   he's ____he is____ or ____he has____

I'm _____   that's_____ or _____

you're _____   it's _____ or _____

we've _____   who's_____ or _____

I've _____   she's _____ or _____

Introducing contractions with **'m, 's, 're, 've**

Contractions: 'm, 's, 're, 've

> 1 📖 Read each sentence.
> 2 ✏️ Write the contraction that completes the sentence.

1. Maria and Rosa say _____ going too.
   | they're they've |

2. _____ seen that movie three times.
   | We're I've |

3. Doug is happy _____ having a party.
   | he's that's |

4. I think _____ older than I am.
   | you're let's |

5. Did you know _____ going to rain?
   | it's we've |

6. _____ made the nicest present!
   | I'm She's |

7. Do you know _____ happening later?
   | what's we're |

8. Sandy thinks _____ a fake ring.
   | let's that's |

9. I hope _____ going to win the prize.
   | we're you've |

10. _____ the girl I saw you with at lunch?
    | We've Who's |

11. _____ all help clean the room.
    | Let's What's |

12. Can't you see that _____ not ready?
    | I'm I've |

Using language arts; using sentence context to select contractions with **'m, 's, 're, 've**

Reviewing Contractions

1 📖 Read the letter.
2 ✏️ Underline the words that can form contractions.
3 ✏️ Rewrite the letter, using contractions in place of the words you underlined.

Dear Mr. Munchos:

I am returning the Handy Homework Helper. It does not work. I have tried many words, but the machine will not form contractions. Your "Helper" is not helping me at all!

My parents say I should not waste my time buying things on cereal boxes. They are right. I have learned my lesson. Please return my $3.00. You can keep the box tops. I do not need them.

Yours truly,
Samantha Brown

Dear Mr. Munchos:

I'm _____

_____

_____

_____

_____

_____

_____

_____

Yours truly,
Samantha Brown

Contractions: 'd, 'll

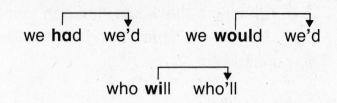
We'd better prepare for landing!

A contraction is made by putting two words together to make one shorter word.

An apostrophe takes the place of the letter or letters that are left out.

we **ha**d → we'd   we **woul**d → we'd

who **wi**ll → who'll

---

1 📖 Read the words below.

2 ✏️ Write the contraction that can be made from the words.

it'll	I'd	they'll	you'd	I'll	she'd
you'll	he'd	we'll	who'd	he'll	they'd

I will _____   they will _____

I had _____   he will _____

you will _____   we will _____

she had _____   they had _____

he would _____   it will _____

you would _____   who would _____

---

1 📖 Read each contraction below.

2 ✏️ Write the two words from which the contraction was made.

he'll _____   they'd _____ or _____

we'll _____   you'd _____ or _____

it'll _____   he'd _____ or _____

you'll _____   I'd _____ or _____

I'll _____   we'd _____ or _____

142

Contractions: 'd, 'll

1. 📖 Read each sentence.
2. ✏️ Write the contraction that completes the sentence.

1. The letter says _____ visit us soon.

> they'll   I'd

2. Alan called to tell us _____ be home late.

> it'll   he'd

3. I thought _____ want to ride your bike.

> you'd   we'll

4. _____ help put the books on the shelf?

> Who'll   I'd

5. _____ never been to that city before.

> I'll   They'd

6. Someday _____ like to travel.

> I'd   it'll

7. Jose wondered _____ taken his pencil.

> you'll   who'd

8. _____ have gone if I had asked her.

> She'd   I'll

9. Do you think _____ ever stop talking?

> he'll   who'd

10. _____ have gone if it hadn't rained.

> We'd   She'll

11. I hope _____ not be too much trouble.

> it'll   who'd

12. _____ have to leave your dog outside.

> It'll   You'll

1 📖 Read the letter.
2 ✏️ Underline the words that can form contractions.
3 ✏️ Rewrite the letter, using contractions in place of the words you underlined.

Dear Peggy Sue,

I am sorry I can not join you for the trip to the pig farm. I have heard that pigs are very smart and that they are also very clean. I know I would enjoy going to the pig farm, but my dog has got fleas and my cat is sick. I will have to go another time. Thanks for inviting me. I am sure you will have fun. It will be an interesting day!

Your friend,
Billy

Dear Peggy Sue,

_____

_____

_____

_____

_____

_____

_____

Your friend,
Billy

Contractions

Directions: Fill in the space next to the contraction that means the same as the words.

Example

can not
- ○ couldn't
- ○ can't
- ○ wouldn't

1. will not ○ wouldn't ○ won't ○ we'll	2. they are ○ they're ○ they'd ○ they'll	3. I am ○ I've ○ I'd ○ I'm	4. have not ○ hasn't ○ hadn't ○ haven't
5. we would ○ we'd ○ we're ○ we've	6. were not ○ wouldn't ○ wasn't ○ weren't	7. do not ○ didn't ○ doesn't ○ don't	8. you had ○ you'd ○ you're ○ you've
9. he has ○ he'd ○ he'll ○ he's	10. you will ○ you'll ○ you've ○ you'd	11. are not ○ hasn't ○ wasn't ○ aren't	12. they have ○ they've ○ they're ○ they'd
13. what has ○ what's ○ what'll ○ wasn't	14. it is ○ it'll ○ it's ○ isn't	15. who will ○ who'll ○ who'd ○ who's	16. she would ○ she's ○ she'd ○ she'll
17. we are ○ we'd ○ we've ○ we're	18. was not ○ won't ○ wasn't ○ weren't	19. I would ○ I'm ○ I'd ○ I've	20. she is ○ she'd ○ shouldn't ○ she's

Plurals: **s**, **es**

THIEVES!

Raccoons and foxes steal berries... Film at 5!

NEWS · NEWS · NEWS

Add **s** to make most words plural.

raccoon   raccoon**s**

In words that end in **ch**, **sh**, **s**, or **x**, add **es**.

fox   fox**es**

In words that end in consonant plus **y**, change **y** to **i** before adding **es**.

berr**y**   berr**ies**

In words that end in a single **f** or **fe**, change **f** or **fe** to **v** before adding **es**.

thie**f**   thie**ves**

1 📖 Read each base word.   2 ✏️ Add the correct ending to make the base word plural. Write the plural on the line.

1. wish   _wishes_

2. city   _____

3. wife   _____

4. match   _____

5. shell   _____

6. tray   _____

7. half   _____

8. ax   _____

9. lady   _____

10. library   _____

11. self   _____

12. inch   _____

13. monkey   _____

14. knife   _____

15. story   _____

16. class   _____

17. wolf   _____

18. radish   _____

146

1 📖 Read each plural word.
2 ✏️ Write its base word on the line.

babies	baby	elves	
birds		puppies	
taxes		benches	
watches		scarves	
brushes		parties	
flies		guesses	
copies		toys	
kisses		names	
loaves		ranches	
donkeys		lives	
leaves		shelves	
cherries		lunches	

Using plural endings: **s, es**; changing **y** to **i**; changing **f** or **fe** to **v**

1 📖 Read each sentence. 2 🔍 Choose the base word from the box that would make sense in the sentence if it were plural.
3 ✏️ Write the plural of the base word on the line.

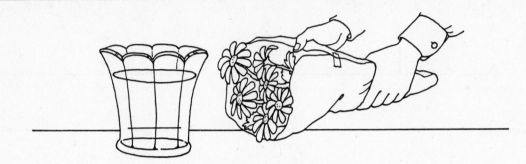

brush	knife	day	box	daisy
monkey	branch	lady	shelf	glass

1. Mom put the pretty bunch of ____daisies____ in the vase of water.

2. Dan wears _____ so he can see the chalkboard.

3. How many _____ are there in a week?

4. The birds were sitting on the _____ of the tree.

5. Please wash all the _____ when you finish painting.

6. We have to build some more _____ for the new books.

7. Those _____ need to be sharpened soon.

8. The _____ in the club went on a hike together.

9. When we moved, we packed all our things in large _____.

10. Did you see any _____ when you visited the zoo?

Unit review: using sentence context to select and spell plural nouns

Plurals

Directions: Read the base word.
Fill in the space next to the plural
for that word.

Example

city
○ citys
○ cities
○ cityes

1. patch	2. loaf	3. boy	4. fox
○ patchs	○ loaves	○ boies	○ foxs
○ patches	○ loafs	○ boys	○ foxies
○ patchies	○ loavs	○ boyes	○ foxes
5. dress	**6. wish**	**7. story**	**8. life**
○ dresses	○ wishs	○ storys	○ lives
○ dresss	○ wishes	○ storyes	○ lifes
○ dressies	○ wishies	○ stories	○ livies
9. fly	**10. bone**	**11. turkey**	**12. dish**
○ flys	○ bonees	○ turkies	○ dishes
○ flyes	○ bonies	○ turkeys	○ dishs
○ flies	○ bones	○ turkeyes	○ dishies
13. half	**14. pencil**	**15. wife**	**16. berry**
○ halfs	○ pencils	○ wifes	○ berrys
○ halves	○ penciles	○ wivs	○ beres
○ halvs	○ pencies	○ wives	○ berries
17. boss	**18. porch**	**19. penny**	**20. ray**
○ bosses	○ porchs	○ pennies	○ rayes
○ boses	○ porches	○ pennys	○ raies
○ bossies	○ porchies	○ pennyes	○ rays

Word Endings:
s, es, ed, ing

Will number 49 drop the ball? He often drops it. Looks like he's dropping it...

Oh no! He dropped it again!

TIGERS

Action words can have the endings **s**, **es**, **ed**, and **ing**.

In words that have a short vowel sound and end in a single consonant, double the final consonant before adding **ed** or **ing**.

drop   drop**s**   dropp**ed**   dropp**ing**

In words that end in **e**, drop the **e** before adding **es**, **ed**, or **ing**.

use   us**es**   us**ed**   us**ing**

In words that end in consonant plus **y**, change the **y** to **i** before adding **es** or **ed**. Do not change the word when you add **ing**.

cry   cri**es**   cri**ed**   cry**ing**

I 📖 Read each base word.
2 ✏️ Add the ending in dark print to the base word. Write the new word on the line.

	s or es	ed	ing
1. clap	claps	clapped	clapping
2. smile			
3. study			
4. fit			
5. close			
6. carry			
7. hug			
8. like			
9. dry			

Introducing inflected endings: **s**, **es**, **ed**, **ing**; doubling the final consonant; dropping the final **e**; changing **y** to **i**

1 📖 Read each action word.
2 ✏️ Write its base word on the line.

saved	save	lining	
jogging		digging	
fried		tried	
diving		grabbed	
dropped		skating	
worrying		buried	
loves		chases	
stepping		moved	
emptied		marries	
dancing		baking	
cuts		knotted	
hurries		spied	

Unit Review: word endings

1 📖 Read each sentence and base word.
2 ✏️ Add **s**, **es**, **ed**, or **ing** to the base word and then write it on the line to complete the sentence.

1. Liz ___studied___ for two hours last night. | study |

2. It's hard to stop _____ my baby sister. | hug |

3. Grandma _____ when we arrived. | smile |

4. I wash the dishes and my sister _____ them. | dry |

5. When the show was over, we _____ loudly. | clap |

6. The neighbors are _____ to another town. | move |

7. Mike _____ in the first row of desks. | sit |

8. That horse is _____ a heavy load! | carry |

9. We _____ at the store for milk. | stop |

10. My friend has a new puppy _____ Rover. | name |

11. Mom _____ to work yesterday morning. | hurry |

12. Our family _____ to have a yearly picnic. | use |

152

Unit review: using sentence context to select and spell words with inflected endings

Word Endings

Directions: Read the base word.
Fill in the space next to the word
with the correct spelling of the
base word and ending.

Example

worry
○ worryed
○ woried
○ worried

1. fit	2. hope	3. like	4. jog
○ fiting ○ fitting ○ fitiing	○ hoping ○ hopping ○ hopeing	○ likied ○ likked ○ liked	○ joged ○ jogged ○ jogied
5. marry	6. try	7. win	8. empty
○ marryes ○ marrys ○ marries	○ tryed ○ tried ○ tryied	○ wining ○ winning ○ winneing	○ emptyes ○ emptyies ○ empties
9. line	10. ride	11. dance	12. tug
○ lined ○ linned ○ linied	○ ridding ○ riding ○ rideing	○ danced ○ dancied ○ dancced	○ tuging ○ tugging ○ tugeing
13. drop	14. grab	15. bury	16. love
○ droping ○ dropping ○ dropiing	○ grabbed ○ grabed ○ grabied	○ burys ○ buryies ○ buries	○ loved ○ lovied ○ lovved
17. knot	18. dive	19. fry	20. bake
○ knoted ○ knotied ○ knotted	○ divving ○ diveing ○ diving	○ fried ○ fryed ○ fryied	○ bakking ○ baking ○ bakeing

Testing inflected endings; using an adapted standardized test format

153

Comparing Words:
er, est

Add **er** or **est** to make some describing words mean "more than" or "most."

    great   great**er**   great**est**

In words that have a short vowel sound and end in a single consonant, double the final consonant before adding **er** or **est**.

    hot   hott**er**   hott**est**

In words that end in **e**, drop the **e** before adding **er** or **est**.

    nice   nic**er**   nic**est**

In words that end in consonant plus **y**, change the **y** to **i** before adding **er** or **est**.

    busy   busi**er**   busi**est**

1 📖 Read each base word.

2 ✏️ Add the ending in dark print to the base word. Write the new word on the line.

	er	**est**
1. small	smaller	smallest
2. large		
3. big		
4. scary		
5. long		
6. wise		
7. happy		
8. flat		

Introducing comparatives: **er**, **est**; doubling the final consonant; dropping the final **e**; changing **y** to **i**

1 📖 Read each pair of sentences.

2 ✏️ Add **er** or **est** to the base word in dark print to complete the second sentence.

1. Elephants are very **heavy** animals.

   Is an elephant _____heavier_____ than a car?

2. It has been **cold** all day today.

   This is the _____ day of the year.

3. This bunch of bananas is **ripe**.

   Which banana is the _____ ?

4. All my clothes got **wet** in the rain.

   I think my shoes are _____ than my socks.

5. My sister went to sleep **early** last night.

   It's the _____ she's gone to sleep all week.

6. That little kitten has such **white** fur!

   Its fur is _____ than snow.

7. Mom likes to run very **fast**.

   She runs _____ than Dad.

8. Look at those **shiny** red shoes!

   They are the _____ shoes I've ever seen.

9. That clown has a very **sad** face.

   He is the _____ clown in the circus.

1 📖 Read each sentence.
2 ✏ Circle the word that makes sense in the sentence.
3 ✏ Write its base word on the line.

1. This must be the hotter (hottest) day of the summer. _____hot_____

2. This store is busier busiest than the one on the corner. _____

3. The movie was longer longest than two hours. _____

4. That is the larger largest dog I have ever seen! _____

5. This plate is flatter flattest than the bowl. _____

6. Rob is always the hungrier hungriest at lunch time. _____

7. Molly is the stronger strongest girl in our class. _____

8. What is the wider widest river in the world? _____

9. That is the stranger strangest story I have ever read. _____

10. My radio is louder loudest than your tape deck. _____

Unit review: using sentence context to select comparatives and identify base words

Comparing Words

Directions: Read the base word. Fill in the space next to the word with the correct spelling of the base word plus **er** or **est**.

Example

tiny

○ tinyer
○ tinier
○ tinyier

1. dim ○ dimer ○ dimmer ○ dimmier	2. smart ○ smarter ○ smartter ○ smartier	3. late ○ lattest ○ latiest ○ latest	4. silly ○ sillyest ○ silliest ○ sillyiest
5. fine ○ finnest ○ fineest ○ finest	6. pretty ○ prettyer ○ prettier ○ prettyier	7. kind ○ kinddest ○ kindiest ○ kindest	8. little ○ littleer ○ littler ○ littller
9. fat ○ fatter ○ fater ○ fateer	10. sweet ○ sweettest ○ sweetest ○ sweetiest	11. brave ○ braver ○ bravier ○ bravver	12. ugly ○ uglyest ○ uglyiest ○ ugliest
13. thin ○ thinest ○ thinnest ○ thineest	14. old ○ older ○ oldder ○ oldeer	15. funny ○ funnyest ○ funniest ○ funnyiest	16. close ○ closer ○ closser ○ clossier
17. easy ○ easyer ○ easyier ○ easier	18. mad ○ madest ○ madiest ○ maddest	19. wise ○ wiser ○ wisser ○ wissier	20. bright ○ brighttest ○ brightest ○ brightiest

Prefixes: dis-, im-, in-, un-

This Shipwreck looks unsafe!

A prefix is a word part that can be added to the beginning of a base word to change its meaning.

The prefix **dis-** can mean "not" or "opposite of."

disable   **dis**agree

The prefixes **im-** and **in-** mean "not."

improper   **in**correct

The prefix **un-** can mean "not" or "to do the opposite."   **un**safe   **un**lock

---

1 📖 Read each base word.
2 ✏️ Add the prefix in dark print and write the new word on the line.

1. **dis-**   like   ___dislike___   trust   _____

2. **im-**   pure   _____   polite   _____

3. **in-**   complete   _____   direct   _____

4. **un-**   plug   _____   fair   _____

---

1 📖 Read each meaning.
2 ✏️ Find the word above with the same meaning and write it on the line.

1. not pure

___impure___

2. not trust

_____

3. do the opposite of "plug"

_____

4. not complete

_____

5. not fair

_____

6. not polite

_____

7. not direct

_____

8. opposite of "to like"

_____

158

Prefixes: mid-, mis-, pre-, re-

The prefix **mid-** means "middle of." **mid**day

The prefix **mis-** means "wrongly." **mis**spell

The prefix **pre-** means "before." **pre**school

The prefix **re-** means "again." **re**fill

---

1 📖 Read each base word.

2 ✏️ Add the prefix in dark print and write the new word on the line.

1. **mid-** night _____   town _____

2. **mis-** read _____   matched _____

3. **pre-** pay _____   cook _____

4. **re-** paint _____   use _____

---

1 📖 Read each meaning.

2 ✏️ Find the word above with the same meaning and write it on the line.

1. middle of night

_____

2. wrongly matched

_____

3. paint again

_____

4. use again

_____

5. read wrongly

_____

6. middle of town

_____

7. cook before

_____

8. pay before

_____

Prefixes:
**dis-, im-, in-, mid-,
mis-, pre-, re-, un-**

1 📖 Read each sentence.
2 ✏️ Circle the prefix that completes the word in each sentence.
3 ✏️ Write the prefix on the line.

1. Did you ever find the book you ___mis___ placed? | mid- (mis-) im-

2. They are _____ building that old house. | re- mid- un-

3. The bird turned around in _____ air. | pre- dis- mid-

4. Tony _____ likes fish too much to eat it. | dis- mis- re-

5. The thief opened the _____ locked front door. | mid- un- im-

6. We could not drink the _____ pure water. | mis- re- im-

7. A report is _____ complete until you finish it. | in- pre- re-

8. _____ heat the oven before baking the bread. | Un- Mis- Pre-

9. Jane _____ tied the knot and opened the box. | re- un- mid-

10. We _____ set our clocks in fall and spring. | dis- in- re-

11. Andy took the most _____ direct way home. | pre- in- mid-

12. This messy room is in great _____ order! | re- dis- pre-

Suffixes: -able, -ful, -less, -ness

A suffix is a word part that can be added to the end of a base word to change its meaning.

The suffix **-able** means "able to" or "able to be."   wash**able**

The suffix **-ful** means "full of."   care**ful**

The suffix **-less** means "without."   use**less**

The suffix **-ness** means "the state of being."   dark**ness**

---

1 📖 Read each base word.
2 ✏️ Add the suffix in dark print and write the new word on the line.

1. **-able**   break _____   accept _____

2. **-ful**   help _____   color _____

3. **-less**   bone _____   hope _____

4. **-ness**   sick _____   still _____

---

1 📖 Read each meaning.
2 ✏️ Find the word above with the same meaning and write it on the line.

1. without hope

_____

2. full of color

_____

3. able to break

_____

4. the state of being sick

_____

5. full of help

_____

6. able to be accepted

_____

7. without bones

_____

8. the state of being still

_____

Introducing suffixes: **-able, -ful, -less, -ness**

161

Suffixes:
-en, -er, -ly, -y

This is my lucky day!

The suffix **-en** can mean "to become."
bright**en**

The suffix **-er** can mean "someone who."
farm**er**

The suffix **-ly** means "in a way."
sad**ly**

The suffix **-y** can mean "full of."
luck**y**

I 📖 Read each base word.
2 ✏️ Add the suffix in dark print and write the new word on the line.

1. **-en**   dark _____   straight _____

2. **-er**   sing _____   teach _____

3. **-ly**   quiet _____   slow _____

4. **-y**   leaf _____   dirt _____

I 📖 Read each meaning.
2 ✏️ Find the word above with the same meaning and write it on the line.

1. full of leaves

_____

2. someone who sings

_____

3. in a slow way

_____

4. to become dark

_____

5. someone who teaches

_____

6. full of dirt

_____

7. to become straight

_____

8. in a quiet way

_____

162

Suffixes:
**-able, -en, -er, -ful,
-less, -ly, -ness, -y**

1 📖 Read each sentence.
2 ✏️ Circle the suffix that completes the word in each sentence.
3 ✏️ Write the suffix on the line.

1. Don was thirst_____ for a glass of water. | -less -y -en

2. We followed our lead_____ up the trail. | -er -ness -ful

3. Add some spices to this taste_____ stew. | -en -ly -less

4. The soft sofa is quite comfort_____ . | -er -able -en

5. Look at the white_____ of the snow! | -ness -able -less

6. Open the shades to bright_____ the room. | -ful -y -en

7. Your pink and blue blouse is color_____ . | -er -ful -less

8. Speak soft_____ so you won't wake her. | -ly -y -able

9. Diane missed school because of ill_____ . | -er -ness -en

10. A garden_____ cares for flowers. | -less -y -er

11. A bee sting can be very pain_____ . | -ful -en -ly

12. Many trees are leaf_____ in the winter. | -able -less -er

Using language arts; using sentence context to complete words
with suffixes: **-able**, **-en**, **-er**, **-ful**, **-less**, **-ly**, **-ness**, **-y**

163

1 📖 Read each sentence.
2 ✏️ Circle the word that makes sense in the sentence.
3 ✏️ Write the word on the line.

1. The ___baker___ mixed the batter to make the bread.

   unbaked (baker) prebaked

2. Can you feel the _____ of the kitten's fur?

   softness   softly   soften

3. Laura thinks the rules of the game are _____ .

   fairly   fairness   unfair

4. I _____ only one word on the test.

   misspelled   speller   spellable

5. Open the window to make the room _____ .

   airless   midair   airy

6. Please fix all the _____ answers.

   correctly   incorrect   recorrect

7. The new boy in our class is very _____ .

   likeable   likeness   dislike

8. Dumping garbage into the lake has made it _____ .

   purely   impure   pureness

9. Timmy's puppy Bobo is very _____ .

   playable   replay   playful

Unit review: using sentence context to select words with prefixes and suffixes

Prefixes and Suffixes

Directions: Read the word. Fill in the space next to its correct meaning.

Example

careful
○ without care
○ full of care
○ able to care

1. **dis**trust	2. train**able**	3. **im**perfect	4. help**ful**
○ not trust	○ train before	○ become perfect	○ full of help
○ trust again	○ train again	○ not perfect	○ help again
○ able to trust	○ able to be trained	○ perfect again	○ without help
5. **in**active	6. bone**less**	7. **un**plug	8. still**ness**
○ active again	○ without bones	○ without plug	○ not still
○ not active	○ full of bones	○ able to plug	○ still again
○ wrongly active	○ before bones	○ do the opposite of "plug"	○ state of being still
9. **mid**day	10. hard**en**	11. **mis**read	12. kind**ly**
○ without day	○ become hard	○ someone who reads	○ in a kind way
○ not day	○ not hard	○ read wrongly	○ not kind
○ middle of day	○ hard before	○ able to read	○ kind before
13. **pre**pay	14. dirt**y**	15. **re**tell	16. teach**er**
○ not pay	○ middle of dirt	○ tell again	○ wrongly teach
○ able to pay	○ full of dirt	○ tell before	○ not teach
○ pay before	○ without dirt	○ not tell	○ someone who teaches
17. **un**made	18. wash**able**	19. sand**y**	20. hope**less**
○ full of made	○ not washed	○ full of sand	○ full of hope
○ not made	○ wash again	○ not sand	○ hope again
○ become made	○ able to be washed	○ middle of sand	○ without hope

Showing Ownership: 's, s'

TAD'S TALENT SHOWCASE featuring: Vern's Violin

To make a singular word show ownership, add **'s**.
That violin belongs to Vern.
That is Vern**'s** violin.

To make a plural word that ends in **s** show ownership, add **'** after the last **s**.
Those caps belong to the boys.
Those are the boys**'** caps.

1 📖 Look at the picture and read each sentence.
2 ✏️ Write a word from the box to complete each sentence.

| books'   bush's   girls'   player's   girl's   book's   bushes'   players' |

1. I like that little ____ girl's ____ smile!

2. The _____ shoes were muddy.

3. The _____ lowest branch was broken.

4. We repaired all the _____ covers.

5. The _____ backpacks were heavy.

6. The _____ shirt was torn.

7. The _____ leaves have all fallen.

8. That _____ last page is missing.

166

Showing Ownership: 's, s'

1 📖 Read each group of words.

2 ✏️ To show ownership, add **'s** or **'** to the underlined word and then write the new group of words on the line.

1. the window of the <u>car</u>   **the car's window**

2. the tails of our <u>cats</u>

3. a toy that belongs to the <u>baby</u>

4. a bat that belongs to the <u>boys</u>

5. the report that <u>Sam</u> wrote

6. the stripes on the <u>zebras</u>

7. the springs in the <u>watches</u>

8. the yards in front of the <u>houses</u>

9. the flowers on the <u>plant</u>

10. the tent used by the <u>campers</u>

11. the heat of the <u>oven</u>

12. the wishes of my <u>mother</u>

1 📖 Read each sentence.
2 ✏️ Write the word that makes sense in the sentence.

1. I like the color of ___Beth's___ sweater. | Beth's   Beths' |

2. Both our _____ houses are green. | friend's   friends' |

3. That one _____ tires are flat. | truck's   trucks' |

4. This _____ prices are low. | store's   stores' |

5. All of these _____ heels are high. | shoe's   shoes' |

6. The two _____ shirts looked new. | brother's   brothers' |

7. Have you seen _____ red scarf? | Ken's   Kens' |

8. _____ shells can be very hard. | Turtle's   Turtles' |

9. My oldest _____ eyes are blue. | sister's   sisters' |

10. The _____ tails are bushy. | fox's   foxes' |

11. _____ boss had a big party. | Dad's   Dads' |

12. Those _____ books are funny. | writer's   writers' |

Unit review: using sentence context to select and write possessives

Showing Ownership

Directions: Read each word. Fill in
the space next to the word that
makes that singular or plural word
show ownership.

Example

pencil

○ pencils
○ pencil's
○ pencils'

1. plane ○ planes' ○ plane's ○ planes	2. captains ○ captains' ○ captain's ○ captains's	3. garden ○ gardens ○ gardens' ○ garden's	4. uncles ○ uncles' ○ uncles's ○ uncle's
5. earth ○ earth's ○ earths ○ earths'	6. girls ○ girl's ○ girls's ○ girls'	7. duck ○ duck's ○ ducks' ○ ducks	8. helpers ○ helper's ○ helpers's ○ helpers'
9. box ○ box's ○ boxs' ○ boxes'	10. kitchen ○ kitchens ○ kitchen's ○ kitchens'	11. maps ○ maps's ○ maps' ○ map's	12. Steve ○ Steve's ○ Steves ○ Steves'
13. officers ○ officer's ○ officers' ○ officers's	14. parade ○ parade's ○ parades' ○ parades	15. matches ○ matches' ○ match'es ○ match's	16. tiger ○ tigers ○ tiger's ○ tigers'
17. windows ○ window's ○ windows's ○ windows'	18. clown ○ clown's ○ clowns ○ clowns'	19. Joan ○ Joans' ○ Joan's ○ Joans	20. kites ○ kites's ○ kite's ○ kites'

Testing possessives; using an adapted standardized test format

Synonyms are words that have almost the same meaning.

rush   hurry

Rush! Hurry! This offer ends at midnight!

TOP 10,000 HITS OF ALL TIME! Only $9.98

1 📖 Read each word.

2 ✏️ Choose a word from the box that is a synonym for that word and write it on the line.

angry	below	cost	dull	forest	frighten	grin	start	ill	keep
large	look	lovely	pick	repair	shop		slice	true	yell	wise

1. mad   angry

2. save _____

3. begin _____

4. woods _____

5. cut _____

6. see _____

7. fix _____

8. sick _____

9. pretty _____

10. smart _____

11. choose _____

12. scare _____

13. boring _____

14. smile _____

15. real _____

16. store _____

17. price _____

18. shout _____

19. under _____

20. huge _____

170

Synonyms

present	large	placed	chilly	started	neat	money	rush
notice	breeze	road	store	purse	dish	couch	movie

1. Diane <u>put</u> the <u>plate</u> on the table.

   Diane placed the dish on the table.

2. You'll have to <u>hurry</u> to get across the <u>street</u>.

   _____

3. Grandma has some <u>coins</u> in her <u>handbag</u>.

   _____

4. There is a <u>big</u> <u>sofa</u> in our living room.

   _____

5. A <u>cold</u> <u>wind</u> blew through the open door.

   _____

6. We got to the <u>film</u> after it had <u>begun</u>.

   _____

7. Did you <u>see</u> how <u>tidy</u> that room is?

   _____

8. Sam bought a <u>gift</u> at the <u>shop</u>.

   _____

Antonyms

Antonyms are words that have almost the opposite meaning.

messy   neat

Let Clyde the Cleaner make your messy room neat.

1 📖 Read each word.

2 ✏️ Choose a word from the box that is an antonym for that word and write it on the line.

thin	short	awake	empty	high	first	front
early	weak	enemy	tight	buy	slow	found
all	laugh	different	dark	left	rough	

1. asleep _____

2. strong _____

3. long _____

4. same _____

5. last _____

6. fast _____

7. smooth _____

8. late _____

9. cry _____

10. low _____

11. fat _____

12. friend _____

13. none _____

14. right _____

15. back _____

16. loose _____

17. sell _____

18. full _____

19. lost _____

20. light _____

Introducing antonyms

1 📖 Read each sentence. 2 ✏️ Underline the word that does not make sense. 3 ✏️ Choose an antonym for the underlined word and write the new sentence on the line.

hot old heavy fix down wet louder over

1. The large rock was too <u>light</u> to carry.

   The large rock was too heavy to carry.

2. My boots got very dry in the rain.

   _____

3. The plane flew under the ocean.

   _____

4. The cold summer sun can make you sweat.

   _____

5. Can you speak softer so I can hear you?

   _____

6. I fell up when I slipped on the ice.

   _____

7. Try to break the lamp that doesn't work.

   _____

8. Rita threw her new shoes in the garbage.

   _____

Homonyms

Just wait until you <u>see</u> the deep blue <u>sea</u>!

TINA'S TROPICAL TOURS

Homonyms are words that sound alike, but have different spellings and meanings.

see   sea

1 📖 Read each word.

2 ✏️ Choose a word from the box that is a homonym for that word and write it on the line.

knot	blue	threw	their	pair	ant	stare
rows	made	write	flour	week	nose	hour
peace	fair	one	sum	steel	prince	

1. piece _____

2. rose _____

3. blew _____

4. weak _____

5. aunt _____

6. right _____

7. won _____

8. maid _____

9. stair _____

10. steal _____

11. through _____

12. some _____

13. pear _____

14. our _____

15. there _____

16. flower _____

17. fare _____

18. knows _____

19. not _____

20. prints _____

174

1 📖 Read each sentence.
2 🔍 Choose a pair of homonyms to complete the sentence.
3 ✏️ Write the sentence on the line.

| blue | rode | seen | their | won | new | hour | Would |
| blew | road | scene | There | one | knew | Our | wood |

1. Dad _____ down the _____ in his new truck.

   Dad rode down the road in his new truck.

2. Cora was the only _____ who _____ a prize.

   _____

3. Jose _____ that I bought a _____ bike.

   _____

4. _____ you chop the _____ for the fire?

   _____

5. Mark _____ out all the _____ candles.

   _____

6. _____ class will be over in one _____ .

   _____

7. _____ are five boys in _____ family.

   _____

8. It's the prettiest _____ we've ever _____ .

   _____

1 📖 Read the words in the box. 2 📖 Read each clue.
3 ✏️ Write the correct word in the puzzle.

eight	angry	young	on	rich	tell	ant	certain	bear	back
dirty	small	loose	by	hear	full	hot	sale		fine	look

ACROSS

1. Synonym for **little**
3. Antonym for **front**
4. Antonym for **clean**
6. Antonym for **empty**
7. Synonym for **see**
8. Synonym for **sure**
10. Homonym for **bare**
11. Homonym for **ate**
14. Homonym for **here**
16. Antonym for **old**

DOWN

1. Homonym for **sail**
2. Antonym for **tight**
3. Homonym for **buy**
5. Antonym for **poor**
6. Synonym for **good**
9. Synonym for **mad**
12. Antonym for **cold**
13. Synonym for **say**
15. Homonym for **aunt**
17. Antonym for **off**

Synonyms, Antonyms, Homonyms

Directions: Fill in the space next to the correct answer.

Example

antonym for **before**
- ○ early
- ○ after
- ○ never

1. synonym for **sad** ○ happy ○ unhappy ○ nice	2. antonym for **freeze** ○ melt ○ cold ○ ice	3. homonym for **sew** ○ soon ○ so ○ son
4. synonym for **tall** ○ high ○ low ○ fat	5. antonym for **heavy** ○ large ○ light ○ small	6. homonym for **cent** ○ sent ○ cell ○ serve
7. synonym for **friend** ○ enemy ○ best ○ pal	8. antonym for **far** ○ away ○ down ○ near	9. homonym for **knew** ○ know ○ now ○ new
10. synonym for **quick** ○ walk ○ slow ○ fast	11. antonym for **sweet** ○ sour ○ honey ○ dry	12. homonym for **meat** ○ mean ○ meet ○ met
13. synonym for **loud** ○ noisy ○ soft ○ warm	14. antonym for **night** ○ dark ○ day ○ shine	15. homonym for **dear** ○ deer ○ dream ○ door

Testing synonyms, antonyms, and homonyms; using an adapted standardized test format

Dictionary Skills: alphabetical order

A B C D E F G H I J K L M N O P Q R S T U V W X Y Z

When you are putting words in alphabetical order, look at the first letters of the words. If the first letters are the same, look at the second letters.

   ↓   ↓   ↓

beige   blue   brown   green

---

1 📖 Read each list of words.
2 ✏️ Number each list in alphabetical order.

1 airplane	___ orange	___ Sam	___ shoes
___ truck	___ pear	___ Lisa	___ slippers
___ car	___ banana	___ Steve	___ skates
___ ship	___ plum	___ Jane	___ socks
___ bus	___ apple	___ Joan	___ sneakers
___ jeep	___ lemon	___ Lee	___ stockings

---

1 📖 Read each list of words.
2 ✏️ Write each list in alphabetical order.

monkey	lion	Bill	_____	goat	_____
lion	_____	Blake	_____	geese	_____
whale	_____	Bob	_____	gull	_____
zebra	_____	Betty	_____	fly	_____
tiger	_____	Bart	_____	fish	_____

178

Introducing dictionary skills; alphabetical sequence by first or second letter

1 📖 Read each shopping list.
2 ✏️ Number each list in alphabetical order.

List 1:
- 4 plates
- ___ napkins
- ___ prizes
- ___ popcorn
- ___ peanuts
- ___ milk

List 2:
- ___ cups
- ___ butter
- ___ balloons
- ___ candles
- ___ bread
- ___ crackers

List 3:
- ___ tape
- ___ ribbon
- ___ string
- ___ snacks
- ___ spoons
- ___ whistle

1 ✏️ Now use all three lists above to write one shopping list in alphabetical order.

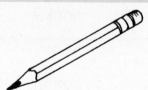

Shopping List

1. balloons
2. _____
3. _____
4. _____
5. _____
6. _____

7. _____
8. _____
9. _____
10. _____
11. _____
12. _____

13. _____
14. _____
15. _____
16. _____
17. _____
18. _____

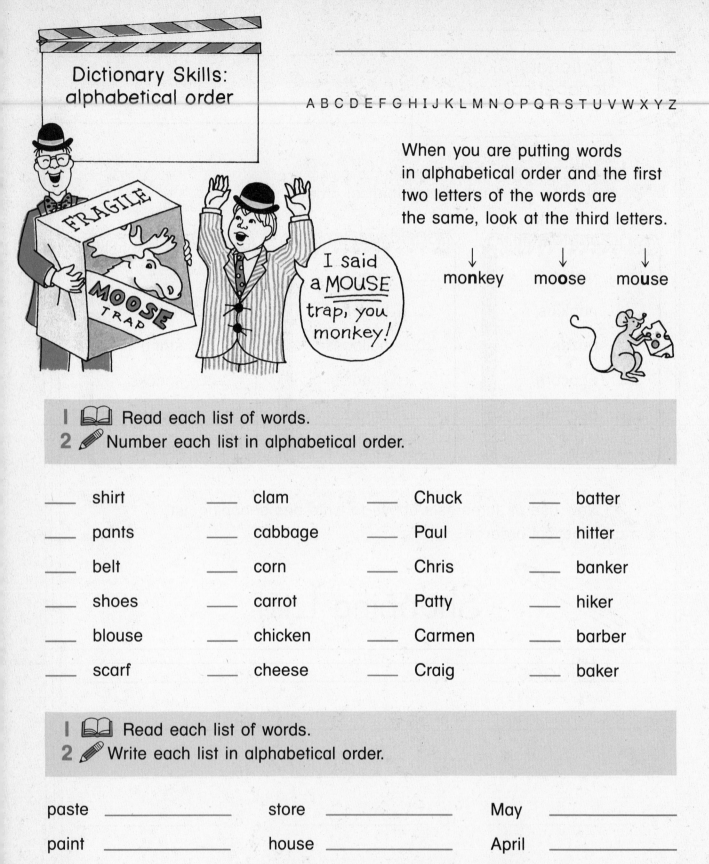

Dictionary Skills: alphabetical order

A B C D E F G H I J K L M N O P Q R S T U V W X Y Z

When you are putting words in alphabetical order and the first two letters of the words are the same, look at the third letters.

↓   ↓   ↓

mo**n**key   mo**o**se   mo**u**se

I said a MOUSE trap, you monkey!

1 📖 Read each list of words.
2 ✏️ Number each list in alphabetical order.

___ shirt	___ clam	___ Chuck	___ batter
___ pants	___ cabbage	___ Paul	___ hitter
___ belt	___ corn	___ Chris	___ banker
___ shoes	___ carrot	___ Patty	___ hiker
___ blouse	___ chicken	___ Carmen	___ barber
___ scarf	___ cheese	___ Craig	___ baker

1 📖 Read each list of words.
2 ✏️ Write each list in alphabetical order.

paste	_____	store	_____	May	_____
paint	_____	house	_____	April	_____
pad	_____	home	_____	June	_____
page	_____	hotel	_____	March	_____
paper	_____	shop	_____	July	_____

180

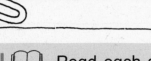

1 📖 Read each shopping list.
2 ✏️ Number each list in alphabetical order.

——— sweater

——— tools

——— soap

——— softball

——— toys

——— socks

——— drum

——— crayons

——— bat

——— dress

——— basket

——— cards

——— markers

——— notepad

——— magnet

——— pencils

——— mask

——— map

1 ✏️ Now use all three lists above to write one shopping list in alphabetical order.

Shopping List

1. _____

2. _____

3. _____

4. _____

5. _____

6. _____

7. _____

8. _____

9. _____

10. _____

11. _____

12. _____

13. _____

14. _____

15. _____

16. _____

17. _____

18. _____

1 📖 Read the words in each box.

2 ✏️ Write the words in alphabetical order to make a sentence.

| ate   awful   Alice |

1. ___Alice___ always _____ an _____ breakfast.

| popcorn   plate   passed |

2. Paco _____ the _____ of _____ .

| dug   yard   dog |

3. The _____ _____ a hole in the _____ .

| snow   fresh   followed |

4. I _____ the footprints in the _____ _____ .

| loud   listen   likes |

5. Laura _____ to _____ to _____ music.

| trash   toy   threw |

6. Who _____ the _____ train in the _____ ?

| George   gift   gave |

7. Gabe _____ _____ a _____ .

182

Dictionary Skills: guide words

Q: What comes between breakfast and lunch?

A: A little brunch!

Guide words are found at the top of each page in a dictionary. They tell you the first and last words on that page. To find a word in the dictionary, decide if it comes in alphabetical order between the two guide words.

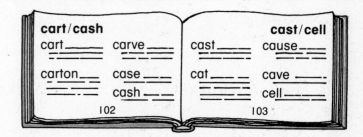

1 📖 Read each pair of guide words.
2 ✏️ Find the word in the box that would come between that pair of guide words in the dictionary and write it on the line.

| coin | kick | scrap | club | knit | say |

key/kid _____kick_____   **save/scale** _____

close/coal _____   **cob/cold** _____

knee/knot _____   **score/sea** _____

1 📖 Read each pair of guide words and the words below them.
2 ✏️ Circle the words that would be found on a dictionary page having that pair of guide words.

finger/flag	**room/row**	**giant/globe**
fill	rope	gift
(five)	rose	glue
first	roll	girl
fish	round	get
fled	rub	glad

Introducing dictionary skills; guide words

Dictionary Skills: guide words

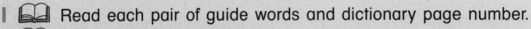

1 📖 Read each pair of guide words and dictionary page number.
2 📖 Read the words below.
3 ✏️ Write the dictionary page number on which you would find each word.

balloon / basket	beat / bike	next / nobody
15	17	72

noise / number	ship / sick	sign / six
73	92	94

1. bed ___page 17___
2. sit _____
3. nine _____
4. shoe _____
5. banana _____
6. north _____
7. shop _____
8. bell _____
9. sister _____
10. not _____
11. silk _____

12. big _____
13. bark _____
14. no _____
15. since _____
16. band _____
17. noodle _____
18. barn _____
19. now _____
20. shut _____
21. night _____
22. beg _____

184

Dictionary Skills: homographs

Even I know this is a duck!

DUCK!!

In the dictionary, you may see two or more entry words that are spelled the same way. These words are **homographs**.

Homographs are words that are spelled alike, but have different meanings.

 duck¹ A bird with a bill and webbed feet.

 duck² To lower the head or bend down quickly.

---

1 📖 Read each pair of homographs and their definitions.

2 ✏️ Write the number of the definition on the line next to the picture that shows its meaning.

---

fly¹   An insect with wings.

fly²   To move through the air.

  2   1

ring¹   A band in the shape of a circle.

ring²   A clear sound like one made by a bell.

 ___   ___

bat¹   A wooden stick used for hitting a ball.

bat²   A small, furry animal that can fly.

 ___   ___

tire¹   To become sleepy.

tire²   A band of rubber around a wheel.

___   ___

pit¹   A hole in the ground.

pit²   The hard seed of some fruits.

  ___   ___

Dictionary Skills: homographs

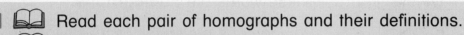

1 📖 Read each pair of homographs and their definitions.
2 📖 Read each sentence below.
3 ✏️ On the line before the sentence, write the number of the definition that has the meaning for the word in dark print.

---

ball¹ Something that is round.
ball² A large party for dancing.

rose¹ A flower.
rose² Stood up.

ground¹ The part of the earth that is land.
ground² Crushed into small pieces.

clip¹ To cut.
clip² Something used to hold things together.

_1_ 1. The kitten played with the **ball** of yarn.

___ 2. That pink **rose** smells so lovely.

___ 3. They **ground** the wheat into flour.

___ 4. Jill kept the papers together with a **clip**.

___ 5. The king and queen went to the fancy **ball**.

___ 6. Everyone **rose** when the president arrived.

___ 7. The **ground** was covered with mud and ice.

___ 8. I need some scissors to **clip** my hair.

186

1 📖 Read each pair of guide words.
2 ✏️ Find the words in the box that would come between that pair of guide words in the dictionary and write them on the lines.
3 ✏️ Number the words in alphabetical order.

| hard | high | had | hold | grow | his | hand | hide |

green/has   **her/home**

___hard___ 4

_____ ___

_____ ___

_____ ___

1 📖 Read each homograph, definition, and pair of sentences below.
2 ✏️ Mark an **X** on the line before the sentence with the same meaning for the homograph as in the definition.

1. **seal**¹ A sea animal.

   ____ Did you **seal** the letter with tape?

   X The **seal** slept on the rocks and swam in the water.

2. **nap**² The soft or fuzzy surface of cloth.

   ____ The **nap** has worn off my old shirt.

   ____ The baby is taking her morning **nap**.

3. **bank**¹ Sloping ground along a river or lake.

   ____ Dad went to the **bank** to get some money.

   ____ We fished from the **bank** of the river.

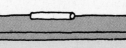

Dictionary Skills

Directions: Read each question. Fill in the space next to the correct answer.

Which word would come <u>first</u> in alphabetical order?

○ person   ○ boy
○ child   ○ girl

---

1. **Which word would come <u>last</u> in alphabetical order?**

   ○ old   ○ who
   ○ many   ○ young

2. **Which word would come <u>first</u> in alphabetical order?**

   ○ take   ○ tell
   ○ two   ○ train

3. **Which word would come <u>last</u> in alphabetical order?**

   ○ hurt   ○ hush
   ○ hut   ○ hunt

4. **Which word would come <u>first</u> in alphabetical order?**

   ○ fish   ○ fix
   ○ first   ○ fit

5. **Which word would you find in the dictionary between the guide words dress / drum?**

   ○ duck   ○ drive
   ○ draw   ○ dog

6. **Which word would you find in the dictionary between the guide words sand / saw?**

   ○ school   ○ same
   ○ save   ○ sack

7. **Which pair of words are homographs?**

   ○ ware, wear   ○ hot, cold
   ○ bat, bat   ○ nice, good

8. **Which pair of words are homographs?**

   ○ off, on   ○ no, know
   ○ high, tall   ○ match, match